SNOWDONIA

Map by Richard Taylor

KEY OVERLEAF

MAP OF SNOWDONIA

KEY TO NUMBERS

Snowdon Group

1. Clogwyn y Garnedd
2. Lliwedd
3. Crib Goch
4. Dinas Mot
5. Clogwyn y Ddysgl and y Person
6. Cyrn Las
7. Clogwyn du'r Arddu
8. Llechog

Glyder Group

9. The Three Cliffs
10. Craig Cwrwgl (Pillar of Elidir)
11. Creigiau Gleision
12. Twll Du (Devil's Kitchen)
13. Upper Cliff of Glyder Fawr
14. Idwal Slabs and Holly-tree Wall
15. Glyder Fach, Main Cliff
16. Tryfan, East Face

Carnedd Group

17. Llech Ddu
18. Ysgolion Duon (Black Ladders)
19. Craig yr Ysfa

Moel Siabod Group

20. Moel Siabod Cliff
21. Moelwyn and Moel yr Hydd Cliffs

Moel Hebog Group

22. Moel Hebog Cliffs
23. Craig y Bere
24. Craig Cwm Silyn
25. Tremadoc Rocks

SNOWDON BIOGRAPHY

Photo by J. R. Edwards

Snowdon

SNOWDON BIOGRAPHY

by

GEOFFREY WINTHROP YOUNG,
GEOFFREY SUTTON,
and
WILFRID NOYCE

Edited by
WILFRID NOYCE

*With 16 pages of photographs
and an endpaper map*

LONDON
J. M. DENT & SONS LTD

CONTENTS

ILLUSTRATIONS

Foreword

THIRTY years ago the late George Lister and I edited a book which surveyed the Snowdon range from almost every viewpoint of human interest. *The Mountains of Snowdonia* went into a second edition some eight years ago through the kind support of Mr John W. Wilson (Crosby Lockwood & Co.) and is now once again out of print with little prospect of revival, owing to the increase in printing costs. It is therefore most timely that an up-to-date review of part of the human story in these mountains should now be undertaken by a team of experts.

Mr Winthrop Young, who spans the whole modern climbing age, from the days of the Victorian pioneers to our own neo-Elizabethan peggers and pitoners, and who gave us his charming chapter on Pen y Pass a generation ago, is here again to look up and down the years as he alone is qualified to do. Mr Sutton, who is now warden of a recreational centre in Derbyshire, the nursery of great rock climbers, and Mr Noyce, whose achievements in the last two decades and whose writings are known and admired the world over, are both splendidly equipped to rewrite the chapters on the literature and climbing of the district, and to bring the story down to the present day.

The Snowdon mountains as a great playground are the theme of this book. It is a tale that begins and ends in speculation. We begin with our vague surmises about ancient times in the mists of old legends: we may imagine our hairy prototypes grunting and groping up the moraines beside the retreating glaciers; or those ancient shepherd warriors, wandering over the Carnedd from their hill-top villages and watching through the cloud breaks for the menace of stranger war canoes beached in the strait to westward; or we may think of the first city-bred visitors, the true forerunners of the twentieth century, the Roman soldiery, swearing and sweating as they built the stockade about their camp beside the infant Llugwy. And when we consider the astonishing changes of recent years and turn to the future, we end in speculation too. Look at the stark, oppressive steepness of the rock walls now conquered light-heartedly by the perfection of technique and daring which blends intimately in the modern rock-climbing genius. In my youth, climbing the 'absolutely perpendicular' was almost wholly confined to those mellow moments at eventide in Pen y Gwryd bar, when the memory of the mere 'it was' was exalted by the genial influence of the tankard. But now not merely is the reality of the perpendicular faced in very deed, but the grim challenge of the overhang, several feet of it, Mr Sutton assures us, on poor holds, is successfully overcome. Will the limit be pushed standard beyond standard, much further up the scale?

> Say that they climb by cloud ways, rope on wings,
> laugh at us old unhappy far-off things?
> Other the boys, other their transient fame.

So wrote the poet thirty years ago—and how right he may be; but his final line, 'Snowdon will look the same,' is less likely, perhaps, to come true after the detonator and the bulldozer have played their part in transforming the district into a reservoir of hydro-electric power to meet the nation's basic material needs. The engineers apart, few really enjoy that prospect. Nor may the beauties and blessings of regimented national forests and national parks grow lovelier with age. God grant we be mistaken.

Let us leave these disturbing fancies, and drawing the curtains together and switching off every mechanical device of sound and vision, let us lose ourselves for a pleasant hour in these pages, while many a precious and precarious moment stirs again in memory, and our mind's eye kindles to look upon the faces of our mountain friends.

H. R. C. CARR.

Preface

MUCH has been written about these our mountains of Snowdonia in a number of their aspects. But no book has taken the *mountaineer* and the most *mountainous* sides of Snowdonia as chief subject. And any such book is bound to include literature in a wider sense within its orbit, since the literature of mountaineering, from which much of our information is drawn, shades imperceptibly into the broader sea of all that has been written in poetry and prose about these peaks.

We believe Snowdonia, small as it is, to be a region in which mountaineering in the true sense and literature (the latter being often the literature of mountaineering) form a striking enough study to warrant a book tracing these two interwoven themes alone. We believe moreover that interest in these hills has never been so great as now. Hundreds of thousands must visit them annually by car and push-bike, by hitch-hike, bus, and on their own two feet. Thousands must climb their rocks; and to these 1956 will seem a propitious year for a summing-up, since the White Slab on Clogwyn du'r Arddu has at last been climbed, its two buttresses and Dinas Cromlech already having been girdle-traversed. There remains no major outstanding rock problem, only a wealth of detail and much on the outlying crags to be explored. Now, therefore, as we all go scrambling up our chosen vertical or swinging the long miles down to our night's youth hostel, seems a good time to stand back a little and ask ourselves: What is it all about? and: How did it all start?

To these questions we have tried, in a brief compass, to give some answer. And this said we must add that we owe an enormous debt to *The Mountains of Snowdonia*, quite apart from our debt to Herbert Carr, its co-editor, for getting us going at all. This second book is his grandchild, and we have with his permission pillaged freely from the first. The plunder is acknowledged, in the main, where it occurs; but we would emphasize the debt, since it shows clearly that this book is a successor of, not rival to, the classic of Carr and Lister.

It may be asked: 'Have you then duplicated?' The answer is: 'Emphatically no!' *The Mountains of Snowdonia* is a comprehensive work, containing many mansions and having many contributors. Most of the mansions we are not qualified to explore. The present book, more streamlined, deliberately leaves out much; not only from lack of specialized knowledge and out of consideration for rising prices, but mainly with the object of presenting a homogeneous portrait, whose subject, when it is not this small, well-known, well-loved group of hills, you will find to be the men and women who frequent them, and who have of course gone on frequenting them since 1948, when Carr's second edition appeared. The Elizabethan botanist; Bingley terrified on the first Welsh rock climb in the eighteenth century and Borrow reciting verses on Snowdon's summit in the nineteenth; the users of club huts and the sleepers in barns or hostels; the bivouac types and those who lie between sheets at comfortable hotels; the hitch-hiking many and the owners of powerful motorcars: they are all here, they or their representatives—what they have said, what they have done, what they have climbed, and what they have written. They are here, pictured by the three of us who have read them, climbed with them, spoken with them. We make no apology for overlaps, since you are seeing them through our three very different pairs of eyes. One of us writes at the age of eighty, with experience of climbing in the last century. Another, in the mid twenties, tells of new developments in which he has taken a part. The third is in the 'middle land' of the late thirties, and we hope even that you will find the variety of our horizons instructive. It is the play of man's changing personality over the static hills that has called this book into being.

Apart from the general debt to *The Mountains of Snowdonia*, we acknowledge our indebtedness to all the many other works without which no history, grave or frivolous, could be compiled: to the journals, the travel books, and the works of the poets, historians, and novelists upon whose writing, and often speaking, we have drawn throughout.

For the photographs, without which this book would be incomplete indeed, we owe a special debt to A. W. Andrews, G. C. Band, A. W. Bridge, J. R. Edwards, J. Gianelli, B. R. Goodfellow, B. Hilton-Jones, E. Langmuir, R. Moseley, D. Ross, and E. A. Wrangham. For the reproduction of the portrait of George Borrow we must acknowledge the permission of the National Portrait Gallery and for quotations, that of Collins Publishers, Faber & Faber, and A. M. Heath Ltd.

Finally, there are four more names that I should like to mention for the help that has been given: Professor T. H. Parry-Williams and Professor J. E. Caerwyn Williams for advice on Welsh literature; and David Cox for his advice and suggestions throughout. Last of all, but not least, we would thank Mr John W. Wilson of Crosby Lockwood & Co. for his kind co-operation over photographs and material borrowed from *The Mountains of Snowdonia*.

WILFRID NOYCE.

Godalming, 1956.

I

Introductory

by

WILFRID NOYCE

Introductory

THE intention of this chapter is to put the general reader in the picture. You may skip it if you like. Where is Snowdonia? What is Snowdonia? How comes this interest in the region? It is not, however, a specialist chapter, although some would say that thoroughly to appreciate Snowdonia you *must* specialize, learning enough of its geology, industry, and natural history to guide your steps and sharpen your eyes. Like the miner-poet, Huw Menai of the Straits, they would be ever

> Shaking the dust from truth. . . .
> Past reading in the hard primeval sod
> The infinite biography of God.

But the climber, with whom we are much concerned, is closer, strange as it may seem, to the poet than to the scientist. He would be more likely to agree with Wordsworth that the geologist (or other specialist for that matter) is

> He who with pocket hammer strikes the edge
> Of luckless rock or prominent stone,
> . . . detaching by the stroke
> A chip or splinter to resolve his doubts:
> And, with a ready answer satisfied,
> The substance classes by some barbarous name
> And hurries on.

Between these two, most travellers will agree that a modicum of detail does not hamper appreciation of the poetic whole; and did not Wordsworth himself end by writing a guide-book? I intend therefore first to take a map and show briefly what kind of country we expect: how it has been built up, how endowed by Nature and how inhabited; next, to return in rather greater detail to its topography, and, since two-thirds of this book are concerned with the climber, to indicate where his chief haunts are, his cliffs and cwms, and how he makes use of them.

Snowdonia is a compact region in the north-west corner of Wales. If you take the map (Endpapers), or better still stand upon Y Wyddfa, the summit of Snowdon, itself, you will be struck by the level appearance of your mountain horizon. Y Wyddfa is *primus inter pares,* yes, but he is not a tyrant. There, eight miles away and only 76 feet lower, is Carnedd Llewelyn. Between lie the Glyders, also doing their best to block the sky-line. All around are pointed or whale-backed summits, rising above tableland and divided from you by deeply cut valleys. This is because, as with Lakeland and the Scottish Highlands, the whole was once a high plain or dome, trenched even as it rose by rivers that have carved out the gorges. What is a little remarkable here is that Nature, with an evident eye for the climber's convenience, cut the whole neatly into five groups of very similar size and character; so that, except on the Carnedds, no crag or summit is really far from the high road.

But I anticipate. This early Miocene period, and the Pliocene age which followed, saw the wearing of the mountains very roughly into the shapes that we know. At the end of the Pliocene age we would have been able, walking in this district, to say: 'That is Snowdon.' The outline was there, but sharper than it is now because it had not yet received the great superficial accumulations that were to come.

The rocks of which this region was composed, and whose formation would have been clearer to the eye then than now, are a vast subject by themselves. If you would learn more, go to Part I, by F. J. North, of *Snowdonia* in the New Naturalist series, where all is explained with diagrams comprehensible to the most Wordsworthian. It is enough here to say that the general structure is synclinal, the dominant trend running north-east to south-west. Walk up the Nant Ffrancon valley and over Ogwen bridge, and you are crossing the core of the first great syncline, seen in the majestic folds of the Devil's Kitchen rocks on your right. Or stand upon the lower slopes of Carnedd Dafydd, at evening especially, and you can see, opposite, the series of beds which slope easily up the west side of Tryfan break sharply over to form its east face, and then reappear again, across the Cwm Tryfan anticline, in the rocks of Gallt yr Ogof.

Much of the rock itself is volcanic, which always used to seem strange to me, as there are no volcanoes, not even extinct ones, among these mountains. The fact is that the lavas must at one time have been not far below the surface, rising for an eruption somewhere. Then, with the wearing of the over-layers, they found themselves at last on top, bedded with sedimentary rocks and traversed, often enough, by dolerite intrusions.

But again I anticipate. The great freeze-up of what we laymen call the Ice Age, but should, resisting a temptation to frivolity, call the Pleistocene period, left as great a mark here as anywhere in Britain. It began about a million years ago. Slowly the land grew colder, the valleys filled with glaciers, the largest those of Ogwen and Llanberis. When warmth returned they retreated and disappeared, leaving a slough of moraine and boulder to mark their passage. It is of interest, in these valleys particularly, for any climber or walker to see the effects of glacial action: here, high upon the sky-line, a huge perched block like that which dominates the Llanberis Pass; there a rounded, smooth, and scoured boiler-plate slab; or again, as in Cwm Tregalan under Y Wyddfa, great lengths of grassy moraine over which the easy walking lies. The lakes, which Borrow on Snowdon summit remarked as the finest feature of the landscape, are also the legacy of the glaciers. Finally and less romantically, the waste land of much of the higher ground is directly due to the badly drained deposits of old moraines.

Warmth, then, returned, and as the final sedimentations settled, the unfrozen streams began again to carve their passage through the rock. The seeds of heather and bracken, trees and flowers, drifted over the land. The Snowdonia of to-day emerged, a region of some twenty by twenty-five miles that still, for all the wearing, holds the highest peaks of southern Britain. It is a compact land, a little aloof, even from the high hills and plains neighbouring it to the east and south. The Denbigh moors are not of it, the shapely Arenig and the long Arans, though they reach almost to 3,000 feet. Neither is Cader Idris, the finest peak to look at outside the area, or the rocky Rhinogs with their high Roman steps. Snowdonia is separate, bounded to the north by the sea, to the west by sea and valley, to the south and south-east

by the valleys of Ffestiniog and Dolwyddelan, to the east by
the wide River Conway. It is different in legend and history
(including climbing history), in climate and industry, even in the
geological clarity with which its story is laid bare for all to read.

To compare Snowdonia with the much larger Lake District is
misleading, and yet inevitable too. If I think of Cumberland, it
is of huge rounded fells, of Grassmoor and Helvellyn and
Skiddaw, or of great bumpy ups and downs of ridge, of Bowfell
and Glaramara and Blencathra. I think of rich valleys, Borrowdale and Buttermere and Grasmere, steep short crags such as Kern
Knotts, and the whitewashed cottages of Langdale. I think of
the Lake poets, of mint cake and rum butter and apple tart teas,
the more delicious when you have spent hours on the misty,
monotonous fells. In North Wales I think rather of the cones or
sharp ridges that the processes of erosion have left; of the broad
mass of the Carnedds, true, but as if they were some great
mammoth-back relic of the primal structure. Mainly it is of the
cone summits such as Y Wyddfa and Y Garn, or the sharp ridges
that look like cones end-on, and that are somehow typical: Crib
Goch and Elidir, Moelwyn and Cnicht and Tryfan. I think of
higher valleys, that drive their barren furrows through the main
ranges, rather than push their noses, as some of the Lakeland
valleys do, into an abrupt cul-de-sac. I think of the boulders and
short grass of Ogwen and Nant Peris, even if I love most the low-
lying wood and sweet meadow of Nant Gwynant (Plate 15) and
the Vale of Ffestiniog. I think of Lliwedd's great thousand-foot
sweep of rock (Plate 7(a)), of slate cottages lashed by misty rain,
of great quarries of slate that seem, in gathering dark, to be themselves mountains piled upon Elidir or the lower Moelwyns by
some giant demon's hand. I think of conflict, of the fighting of
Arthur and Llewelyn, Dafydd and Glyndwr, against the accursed
Saxon. I think of wars and bards and miners, and of the
observance of the sabbath; but also of the Snowdon Railway
(recently televised) valiantly chugging its load of Sunday tourists
to Snowdon summit. Yes, and I have known rock climbers who
were not above taking a lift.

I have said that the valleys of Snowdonia which finally emerged
are higher-based than those of Cumberland. This gives the land

a sterner look, appropriate to its restless past.   Short grass covers
the bouldery slope, varied with bracken and heather and bilberry.
But there is not the Scottish luxuriance of gayest heather that seems
instinct with wild life.   Flowers there are, but you must keep an
eye open for them.   Even the woodland species, primrose and
wood anemone, have penetrated far into the hills.   Clogwyn du'r
Arddu, to the north of Y Wyddfa, and the great dripping limestone of Twll Du are favourite hunting-grounds.   On the latter,
just right of the Devil's Kitchen, some thirty different species can
be picked out at one 'sitting,' including the famous *Lloydia*.
This region, by some trick of Nature, is the only one in Britain
which boasts *Lloydia*; and these cliffs will always be associated
with it by any who have seen its pale beauty upon some high dark
ledge of the 'hanging gardens.'   In a similar vein, but less
pleasantly, some climbs are associated with *Andreaea*, the rock
moss that can crumble at a touch and powder the climber's eyes;
and a gully on Crib y Ddysgl was named, by someone unfortunate enough to climb it in summer, from its luxuriance of parsley
fern.   Indeed there is a plant aroma in the naming of many rock
climbs, and their description.   'Best when the fruits are ripe,'
Menlove Edwards wrote of one of them, and there will always be
Heather Terrace, Yew Buttress, Holly Route, Rowan Route,
Sylvan Traverse, Ivy Chimney, and Whinberry Route to testify
to the vegetable association.

Most of these, admittedly, are low down, for the higher Snowdonia is no longer famed for the trees said to have once adorned
its flanks.   It is too wet and windy.   In climate, as in other ways,
the region is distinct from those that surround it.   In general it
shares the wet, mild climate of all western coastal regions, and the
mountains, as always, receive the first buffetings of the prevailing
south-west winds.   Warm damp air, as we were taught in our
first geographies, rises on meeting the colder land, the cloud which
all climbers know is produced, and rain falls.   The average yearly
fall in Cwm Dyli under Snowdon is 157 inches, while at Caernarvon, only a few miles away, it is no more than 30 inches, and
at Llandudno to the north-east even less.

This does not mean that 'the rain it raineth every day.'
Simply that when it does rain, it usually rains harder than

anywhere else.   For fine days, if cloudy, Snowdonia is as well off as most parts, and my impression is that we do better nowadays than the pioneers, whose accounts bristle with weeks of continuous downpour such as I, for one, have seldom experienced, and never since the Second World War.   August, the holiday month, is the wettest, along with the months from October to January inclusive. But even in January I have had five days of continuous gym-shoe climbing, and in April, the driest month with May, June, and September, a fortnight almost cloudless.   Even when it is raining hard on the higher summits, it is often strangely easy to escape into sunshine at Cwm Silyn or on the increasingly popular bluffs above Tremadoc village, which are out of the main line of onslaught.

Snowdon: the Peak of Snow.   Early travellers believed it to be snow-covered all the year round.   In fact, of course, as Dafydd ap Gwilim recorded in a poem in the fourteenth century, it is December or January that usually brings the change from rain to snow.   For the next three months even the ordinary paths can be very slippery, serious undertakings, the ice gullies a joy to the climber and the slopes of Carnedd or Siabod to the skier. In 1951 the number of ill-shod, unprepared walkers stranded at the summit hotel was a record, as was also the number of rescues performed by the team of which C. R. Briggs, of Pen y Gwryd, is in charge.   But it is then, in winter, that the mountains are most truly themselves, and most truly mountains.   The big crowds have gone; the snow shapes have kept themselves for this season, to be shown to the mountaineer alone.   Him they buffet and toss through the short misty day; but at evening, as he descends, a strange sun sword lights the murk: suddenly all the ranges from Arenig to Cader Idris lie there revealed, shining in a golden armour.   Then it is that he loves them, knowing this to be his reward for the labour of cutting steps, of finding and losing the way, that has gone before.

Even in January, however, the hills may be quite bare of snow; and by April it is usually gone.   It lingers longest, sometimes into July, on the northern slopes of Carnedd Llewelyn and in the Parsley Fern Gully of Crib y Ddysgl.

Many benightments in the winter months could be avoided

with common sense and a knowledge of the local weather conditions. Everybody should know that a pale sunset, a halo round the moon, unusual clearness of view (to see the Isle of Man or Ireland is usually a bad sign), gusty winds, or a 'shiny' effect on the rocks—all are ominous. A north wind is good, as in the Alps, an east wind generally cloud-laden—for Snowdonia is very cloudy—but dry; west and north-westerly winds are showery and cool, but not usually continuous in their raining. It is the south-west wind, of course, that brings the heavy falls. But when you have looked at all the signs, remember that there are always exceptions.

This is the land, and of its story, or rather the story of our human connection with it, you are going to hear something in the next chapters. Its people are the Welsh, and their names are Williams and Jones and Hughes. Its other denizens, apart from the occasional Sassenachs, are the fox and the hare, the raven and the peregrine, the buzzard too sometimes, and the wheatear; but above all the sheep, farmed all over the rough hills and found occasionally on the cliffs themselves. The lower valleys are grazed by the black cattle of Wales, and the farmers are a sturdy race. But the great industry, developed from the late eighteenth century, is slate. Copper is no longer mined, though it has left its scars in the Glaslyn and Nantlle hollows. But slate, as anyone can see who walks the road and looks at the houses, still prospers, in a form less expansive than during the last century. The great beds that wriggle their way under Elidir Fawr have surfaced in the biggest quarries in the world, Penrhyn Quarry near Bethesda and Dinorwic Quarry above Llanberis, on the opposite side. At Blaenau Ffestiniog, where the strata are less steeply inclined, the workings are in mines, again some of the biggest in the world. These account for the huge heaps of waste that do their best to disfigure the lower Moelwyns.

This is a land of slate, of great grey intrusions among the pointed peaks. A land of dew-tipped grass and grey cliffs, of rounded stone walls against which the sheep huddle in the rain. A land where the miners are kindly and the shepherds, if you can get to know them and not be rebuffed by a suspicion that is old as the English, generous as they are strong. May they never be driven into the sea by the second (climber and tourist) invasion of the Saxon hordes!

It is this land that we are going to explore.

2

Anybody driving from Bangor, over a fine week-end, and stopping at the tenth milestone along the A5 road, will see a strange sight. Some two hundred yards from him, up on the right, a rock buttress noses its way down the lower slopes of a heathery mountain, to lose itself among giant boulders below. The crest is curiously white against the grey of the remainder. All over it, in various attitudes, he will see groups of people, of both sexes, dressed in shorts or trousers, shirts or anoraks, gym shoes or boots. They seem to be moving haphazardly, and there will be a good deal of shouting. If he looks closer he will see that they are in separate parties, one person above the other. The leader of one party has advanced to a heathery-looking ledge; he has tied himself on to something, a projection of rock perhaps, invisible from the road. Number Two is ascending, the rope is being drawn in, advice is being shouted from above.

'There's a good press-up for your left hand, just round the corner.'

'What's that?'

'THERE'S A GOOD PRESS-UP . . .'

'Oh, I *see*!'

'If you could get your left foot somewhere near where your right hip is, and step up . . .' says Number Three from below helpfully. And so on. At last Number Two is there. It is his turn to shout advice to Number Three. Now they are all on the ledge. The leader goes on. . . .

This sport of rock climbing, with which a good deal of our book is concerned, occupies thousands of men and women, girls and boys, over much of the year. You are going to hear of its origins and early history in Snowdonia, of later developments, and finally something of those who have written about it, and about many other aspects of the Snowdonian scene. It would therefore perhaps be well to be clear about the cliffs and hills where it is practised; and I will try now to give a brief topography, which may be skipped by the expert or used in conjunction with the diagram and key (Endpapers) by those not so sure of themselves. But I add 'hills' to 'cliffs,' because very few climbers would want rock climbing to be the whole game, and I can start with a word on walking. In the great sport of mountaineering there are, thank heaven, no rules, and only one absolutely general principle, that of 'getting up.' We are all different, thank heaven for that too, and we prefer mixing our methods of getting up in differing proportions. Some of those you see upon the Milestone Buttress will go on round to the East Face of Tryfan, climb a buttress and on over the Glyders, perhaps to finish at the Devil's Kitchen. Some, preferring the more highly spiced dish of pure technique, may go on to the East and West Walls of the Idwal Slabs. Some of the best rock climbers to-day can spend a week on, say, the Three Cliffs of Llanberis, Dinas Mot, and Cyrn Las, without going once to the top of a mountain.

But to some of these the finest mixture will be that of days, or weeks, spent on slab and corner, with other days of long walking over the summits. That is, perhaps, the best way to know Snowdonia both in detail and as a whole. Start at Bettws y Coed to the east, and walk over the tops to finish at Nantlle in the west. Or do the three-day route from Helyg over the Glyders and Siabod to Ffestiniog. Thence over the Rhinogs to Dolgelley, and as tail-piece Cader Idris and the Arans down to Bala. To these walkers the walk of the fourteen three-thousanders will be an attraction. The fastest time I do not mention, for fear of stimulating competition; but thirteen hours is reckoned a good average time from Beddgelert to Conway. It is a walk of great charm, over a variety of types of ground from the rocky Snowdon ridges, across the mixed ground of the Glyders to the broad hump of Foel Fras in the Carnedds. A mist adds to the hazards, and to the time.

But to return to our muttons. The walker, with stout footwear and a good map and compass, can take care of himself. He lays out his map, chooses a pleasant round, and follows it. The climber, from that legendary parson onward, has sought out and gradually mapped for himself the steep cliff faces where he finds his pleasure and delight.

These cliffs are taken in the order in which they are given in the key to the diagram on the Endpapers. And I would emphasize that they are the principal cliffs only, for this is not a guide-book, or they are those mentioned later in the text.

I. SNOWDON GROUP

1. *Clogwyn y Garnedd* (Frontispiece)

The west and north-west facing cliff under Y Wyddfa above Cwm Dyli. It is of no interest to the pure rock climber, being loose, vegetational, and strewn with débris from the former summit huts. But it is fine to look at and the gullies in winter give 500 feet and more of steep snow and ice climbing, the best in Wales.

2. *Lliwedd* (Plate 7(*a*))

The eastern arm of Snowdon has upon its northern flank the biggest cliff of the district, 1,000 feet from top to bottom of the West Peak. Mainly felstone, some volcanic ash. A characteristic feature is the grooving, which gives 'Lliwedd flavour' to the harder climbs, particularly those on the lower slope of the East Buttress. The special hunting-ground of the Pen y Gwryd and Pen y Pass groups, it is now considered, except for Central Gully, an accessible cliff. The routes have tradition and a fine mountaineering tang. They demand good route-finding.

3. *Crib Goch*

Splendid to look at, with its serrated pinnacle top. Dropping to the north-west is one good buttress nearly 250 feet high, which has three routes. Elsewhere the rock, upper lava geologically, is friable.

4. *Dinas Mot*

The gable end of North Ridge of Crib Goch, 400 feet high and its base as low as the 1,000-foot contour. The smooth, well-defined (volcanic) 'Nose' holds a network of hard routes. Around the Nose is dolerite intrusion full of heathery climbs.

5. *Clogwyn y Ddysgl and y Person*

From the ridge of Crib y Ddysgl a rock promontory juts north into Cwm Glas. Its left side drops steeply—Clogwyn y Ddysgl. It ends in the 'Parson's Nose.' The cliffs are high, and can be cold. Rock sometimes firm volcanic, but with basalt 'organ pipes' in places. Longest climb some 350 feet.

6. *Cyrn Las*

A most impressive 600 feet of rock, at the head of lower Cwm Glas. About 1,500 feet up. Long condemned as rotten, its volcanic parts have some splendid, long, mountaineering routes, very exposed.

7. *Clogwyn du'r Arddu* (Plate 9)

The experts' Mecca. Very well marked synclinal structure, the East and West Terraces hemming the West Buttress of 400–500 feet, whose character is of overlying slabs slanting left. The East Buttress, a perfect triangle, is split by great vertical cracks. The cliff ends at 2,500 feet on the north-east shoulder of Snowdon.

8. *Llechog*

An indefinite, disappointing cliff on the south-west arm of Snowdon, where it curls round.

II. Glyder Group

9. *The Three Cliffs*

These three small but sharply defined cliffs, with Craig Ddu to their west, face Snowdon across the Llanberis Pass. They are very low down, being only a few hundred feet from the road. Dinas Cromlech (Plate 8) faces up the valley. It is the tallest (300 feet) and split by spectacular cracks. Carreg Wastad and Clogwyn y Grochan, the widest, also have some of the hardest climbs hereabouts. Craig Ddu (Plate 6(a)) is here too.

10. *Craig Cwrwgl (or Pillar of Elidir)*

A small boat-shaped cliff on the breast of grassy Elidir Fawr to north-east of summit. It can well be taken with a walk.

11. *Creigiau Gleision*

An indefinite and once overrated limestone-type cliff on the east side of Foel Goch above the Nant Ffrancon.

12. *Twll Du (or Clogwyn y Geifr)*

The splendid calcareous cliffs of the great synclinal fold, above Llyn Idwal and between Glyder Fawr and Y Garn.   About 400 feet high, and 1,500 feet up.   Apart from the Devil's Kitchen (Plate 7(*b*)), Staircase, and Hanging Garden Gully, the cliffs are little visited owing to dampness, loose rock, and vegetation— which however make them a botanist's hunting-ground.

13. *Upper Cliff, Glyder Fawr*

The south-east end of the circle of cliffs heading Idwal.   High on the mountain.   Climbing mainly of the old type, apart from the 'Grey Group.'   The climbs land you near the bare summit plateau of the higher Glyder, all boulder-strewn.   Volcanic rock.

14. *Idwal Slabs and Holly-tree Wall*

Climbs for Everyman.   The slabs are of volcanic rock, possibly glacier-worn; a 400-foot sweep at an angle of 45 degrees.   On the left drops the steeper East Wall, above is another steep con- tinuation.   Climbs range from the classic slab routes to 'Suicide Wall.'   The start is low down, near Idwal Lake, and the place most popular.

15. *Glyder Fach*

An irregular but very definite cliff face, 2,500 feet up, on the northern flank of the mountain above Bochlwyd.   Firm volcanic rock similar to that of the great summit monoliths. Fine climbing.

16. *Tryfan* (Plate 14(*b*))

The most popular climbing ground in Wales.   The series of volcanic and sedimentary beds which breaks off to form the East Face is jointed the right way, giving big ledges, good holds, and short pitches.   The climbing face above Heather Terrace is about 500 feet.   At the western tip of the North Ridge, a short way above the A5 road, is Milestone Buttress.   The Terrace Wall on the North Buttress is steeper than the rest. Tryfan's popularity is partly due to the singular form and quaint symmetry of the whole mountain.

III. Carnedd Group

17. *Llech Ddu*

A steep gable-shaped cliff low down on the northern arm of Carnedd Dafydd, above Cwm Llafar. Little visited, but it has a fine 420-foot route, Central Route.

18. *Ysgolion Duon (or Black Ladders)*

A big cliff, steep and broken, formed from a thick sheet of dolerite on the northern side of the Carnedd Dafydd ridge, east of the summit. Western Gully is 900 feet and the best climb. Not often visited; it involves a longer walk than is usual in Snowdonia, over typically grassy Carnedd ground.

19. *Craig yr Ysfa*

The most popular cliff on the Carnedds, on the north-east shoulder of Carnedd Llewelyn. Great Gully is 800 feet. The rock is volcanic, but easily angled and often heathery. The hardest and increasingly popular climbs are on the walls of the Amphitheatre, Cirque, etc., the big hollows.

IV. Moel Siabod Group

20. *Moel Siabod Cliff*

The summit and spurs of Siabod are of dolerite. The south-facing cliff above the lake has some buttress climbing, not of a high order.

21. *Moelwyn and Moel yr Hydd*

These volcanic rocks facing south-east have become increasingly popular. The buttresses are of 200–300 feet and are being explored. Approach by Blaenau Ffestiniog and Tan y Grisiau. A good walk on over the Moelwyns or Cnicht.

V. Moel Hebog Group

22. *Moel Hebog Cliffs*

The east-facing cliffs, composed of rhyolite and overlooking Beddgelert, have fairly recently been found to have some reasonable climbs, some of them 300–400 feet. The climbs land you near the top of Hebog, a massive and majestic mountain (Plate 15).

23. *Craig y Bere*

A south-facing cliff on the flank of Mynydd Mawr. The rock is mainly sound granite, with friable intrusions. Angel Pavement, the longest and most popular climb, is 500 feet.

24. *Craig Cwm Silyn*

A fine group of rocks, some 1,500 feet up, above Nantlle. Best known is the Great Slab, 300 feet, on which are several hard routes besides two easier classics. Often sun-drenched when the higher hills have rain.

25. *Tremadoc Rocks*

A series of bluffs, 150–200 feet high, composed of steep dolerite on a substratum of shale, almost at sea level and just by the road near Tremadoc village. They face south and have almost no rain. Scorned by the purists, they have become an experts' playground for wet days—and even dry ones.

II

From Genesis to Numbers

(*from the early climbers
to the 1920's*)

by

GEOFFREY WINTHROP YOUNG

From Genesis to Numbers

I

King Arthur yoed up to the creste of the cragge, and than he comforted himself with the colde winde.

Sir Thomas Malory.

There can be little doubt that this is the first recorded ascent upon rock in Wales; and King Arthur's close connection with the Bwlch y Saethau makes it presumable that the crag was upon Lliwedd. Sir Thomas Malory, the first master of English prose, compresses into this moving sentence all the elements that make up a good climb: its successful completion, the personal reaction of the climber, and his motive. All of us who are mountaineers have sought that comfort from the 'creste,' and have found our right sense of proportion restored by 'the colde winde' over the pass.

Climbing has always been a competitive outlet for young masculine agility. Although records are lacking, there can never have been a break in crag climbing, or scrambling as it used to be called, by the young of every hill generation, the cave boys and the herds. But in the history of every game or skill a moment came when the activity became conscious, when it began to take form, with local rules, and emerged as a sport. The skirmish along the lane with a round stone or a ball, between indefinite numbers from rival villages, at such a moment of general realization became football; the knock-up between chapel buttresses took form as fives.

In the same way, mountaineering emerged in the course of the nineteenth century as a sport with a name; and the age-long anonymous scrambling took definite shape as rock climbing, within the memory of those of us who frequented mountain regions at the end of the century. We had been drawn to the hills by the combination of beauty and adventure which they presented in a safe and prosperous era, and we were held by the fascination we discovered in pitting our strength against their steepness and uncertainty, because it is the uncertainty of the issue which lends charm to every fashion of human contest.   We took each difficulty or 'pitch' at its own value, and solved it by natural agility, rarely noticing enough in the struggle to be able to say afterwards how we had done it.   The fact that the 'Thank-God' hold on Lliwedd and the little finger-touch on the Pillar Nose were particularized is significant.   The only techniques recognized were Alpine, cutting steps or testing snow.   We looked to a few men born with nerve and agility to be the leaders on our climbs.   That there could be a technique or principles generally applicable on *rock* did not occur to anyone at first; rock difficulties appeared as various as the physiques of the men who climbed the rocks.   A climb was a personal contest with a series of always different rock problems.

It is only recently that the word climbing has come to suggest a skill; at first it described what we now call hill walking.   Climbing on rock was termed scrambling, a word which has lost its dignity in spite of Whymper's famous title.   This scrambling, on English, Welsh, or Scottish rocks, was as old as the hills.   It was not imported from the Alps by the returning Alpine pioneers; but it received from their new mountaineering enthusiasm the impetus that in a few years caused it to emerge as rock climbing, as a separate skill of its own.

There could be no records or recognized rock routes before this happened.   The feats of the cave man and the lonely herd, the squire's and the parson's son, are lost in the silence of time and the hills.   Even when mountaineering took form as a sport in the nineteenth century, the pride of the first pioneers ordained that no practice other than Alpine climbing should be accepted as mountaineering.   I was misled myself by this exclusiveness into writing that our Alpine predecessors who went winter holidaying and scrambling in Britain did so only as training for their serious Alpine mountaineering.   No doubt the Alps held their chief interest, just as the new age finds its highest realization in the Himalayan ranges.   But the climbing on the home cliffs to which they happily returned was not only training for the Alps, which was the excuse enforced by the already dominant traditions of the first Alpine fraternity. In fact it was to revive a youthful and native enjoyment.

The feeling for mountains, the strange attraction they have had for a number of men through all ages, must always have demanded active expression. So far as literary allusions can help us, we can observe the small but inevitable procession among the mountain lovers. First to approach mountains with awe and walk among them with every precaution. Then to ascend their terrors with conscious heroism, and an awakening appreciation of their beauty. Finally to penetrate their sanctuaries, brave their bolder ridges, and even climb their precipices. This last stage could not be reached until transport and familiarity had dispelled the dark clouds of mystery and tradition which defended our hill tops as densely as the spirits of superstition still infested the high Alps in living memory. Hills kept their obscurity very late in time. They were rarely approved for other than their flowers or birds or streams and utilitarian waterfalls. Their pertinent vocabulary contained little but 'wild,' 'savage,' 'horrid,' and the like survivals of primitive hauntings and terrors. Only occasional and surprising references in history betray a continuous human and hidden relationship to them: Alexander the Great, ending his campaigns and life in the Himalaya, after scaling the Sogdiana pinnacle by the help of rope-slings and stirrups, the first recorded mechanical aids; the African deserters in Spain in 200 B.C. using iron pitons on rocks, as Livy reports; the Emperor Majorian crossing the Alps with the help of ice-axes, as described by Apollinaris Sidonius in A.D. 458; or the Tyrolese, in the Middle Ages, 'climbing places only known to themselves' on crampons attached to their hands and knees, in La Colonie's account.

In the Welsh mountains we cannot be said to begin recorded history until the age when men began to travel in earnest, and to publish their adventures. In 1536 John Leland made the first of these *Itineraries*, with lists of the Welsh lakes and mountains. He held the traditional Greek attitude that mountains are divisions between peoples, and valuable only as sources of springs and rivers and so of fertility. Eryri [1] to him was 'horrible with the

---

[1] Heremi, Heriri, or Eryri, signifying eagle rock, means the Mountains of Snowdonia.

sighte of bare stones,' and we remember that the Pillar Rock remained the Pillar Stone until this century. William Camden in 1586 followed the lead of the geographers, in his *Britannia,* and he adopted the notable explanation that Nature 'reared mountains to bind the Island fast to the bowels of the earth,' which seems to echo 'planted their roots in the sea.' There followed the early map-makers, a class by themselves. John Speed, in 1610, paraphrased Camden, and caught the Shakespearian tone in terming these 'mountaines the British Alpes.' The claims of science succeeded those of geography. In 1639, under the screen of botanizing, Thomas Johnson made the first recorded ascents since King Arthur. He had still to be 'horror-stricken' by the precipices, but like a good mountaineer he ate his provisions in thick clouds on the summit in the right Snowdon manner. He only failed to reach the top of Carnedd Llewelyn because his guide suffered from the contemporary fear of 'eagles and isles and uncompanioned peaks.'

Other botanists and active inquirers followed his tracks. But the first to write with what we feel to be first-hand knowledge of the summits was Edward Llwyd, keeper of the Ashmolean. He first drew attention to the rock castle crowning Glyder Fach, and made the discovery that the top of a mountain usually recedes as fast as we surmount its successive profiles.

By the mid-eighteenth century it became permissible to allege other reasons than science as motives for mountain visits; although science remained up the climber's sleeve as a trump card for the public until Leslie Stephen's mocking exposure of its pretence. Health provided as decent a cover for Lord George Lyttleton when he toured through Wales and climbed Moel Hebog. He made the discovery that there was merit in the colour over the sea, and even 'much savage beauty in the vales.' He thus preserved 'a stock of health that may last all the winter.' By 1770 Joseph Cradock was free to steep himself in the emotions rather than in the sciences; he could find in the 'disjointed rocks, black caverns, and issuing cataracts of Aber-Glaslyn the noblest specimen of the Finely Horrid the eye can possibly behold.'

The great Dr Johnson, disappointed of making his own journey right through Wales, found Thomas Pennant in his *Journey*

1. 'View in Nantberis.' (From the engraving by Moses Griffith, in Pennant's *Tour in Wales*, 1781)

to Snowdon (1781) the 'best traveller I ever read.' A Welshman and a keen mountaineer, Pennant could describe peaks as well as he could climb them. He first made use of the term Snowdonia, and gave it authority. Pennant, and his energetic and clear directory, attracted a flood of imitators and followers, on foot and with the pen. The scientist-pedestrians were now leavened by journalists intent upon topography for tourists. But descriptive writing was still content with climbing generalities and the traditional timidity, or 'horror.' 'The severest labour in my whole life!' and the like phrases, had still to misrepresent an adventure so enjoyable that it was worth writing up sensationally for public consumption. But William Hutton, by 1790, had got so far towards control of the situation and of his nerves that he could record something of 'how' he climbed. He remarked that, if a man falls while ascending, it must be upon his hands; but if in descending it will be upon his back. That anyone, in climbing, might even fall upon his feet, no one had yet dared to mention.

At the end of the eighteenth century we are given a sudden glimpse of what may have been going on behind the screen of mountains, and of convention, since Arthur, Alexander, and Apollinaris, and certainly since Captain Bingham in 1580 'climbed a crag to fetch down an eagle.' Two clergymen, Peter Williams of Llanberis, who acted as an amateur guide to the hills, and William Bingley, a professed botanist, in 1798 not only made the first recognized rock climb in the region, on the eastern terrace of Clogwyn du'r Arddu, but they described the use of hands and knees (to climb with and not merely to fall upon), the sensation of a loosening hold, nails in their shoes, and even the use of a belt as a belay or handhold. On the way up Tryfan, also, from Cwm Bochlwyd, Bingley noted that they had to 'use their hands every half-dozen steps.' A century later, when my father led two of his small sons up that route, so little even then was any track indicated or traces left upon the rocks that I recall having to use my hands quite as often as Bingley.

A period followed when we hear only of increasing tourist penetration up the valleys, and of night ascents of Snowdon for the sake of the sunrise view. This was a very blind byway in mountaineering, and led nowhere.   But it is remarkable, in this half-century of the soul's awakening to scenery and the pictur-esque, how complacently discomfort was accepted on the road to the discovery of beauty.   Rude hillsides are at their worst through the hours of darkness, and the yawns and chills of sleeplessness before dawn formed a heartless preparation for any appreciation of the everyday miracle.   A mist as unrevealing as this darkness enshrouds the feats of the early exploratory scramblers, who were the night-walkers' contemporaries.

With romanticism and the nineteenth century, roads began to creep up the most secret valleys and over the finely horrid passes. Path-pedestrians could tramp and coaches could advance into the hearts of hills.   A few Welsh mountain names became familiar and current, and the mountains belonging to them became there-fore safe and even worth while.   Small guest-farms and inns appeared in the recesses; and around them, for a short and singular phase, shepherd-guides and even mountain ponies flourished, acting as supports and props to venturesome men and women during the years of mountain initiation.

It was the independent and original minds which came first; and writers have an advantage in history in that their trails are printed and their names survive.   Shelley wandered into, and out of, these mountains, and it was the memory of their innate beauty rather than of their traditional terrors which again and again gives light and shadow in his poetry.   George Borrow in *Wild Wales* detailed a far closer notion of the mountain forms; but his admira-tion was still from the mountain's foot.   A little time passed, and Charles Kingsley, Tom Taylor, and Tom Hughes were depicting the coming of the anglers and of the trampers.[1]

Through the years the long-striding academic hill trampers were advancing deeper, and higher; and some of them no doubt became scramblers.   By the 1850's our returning Alpine pioneers had started to chase their new mountain enthusiasm into their home hills, and they brought with them their innovation of recording exploits in diaries and even journals, so that we begin to learn something of their predecessors, the nameless wanderers, oddities,

[1] See pages 133, 138, and 144 for the writings of the authors in this paragraph on Snowdonia.

and recluses whom they found already frequenting the mountain recesses and taking to scrambling. Characters appear such as the veteran Parson Jackson of the Pillar Stone, and the unknown cleric after whom the Parson's Nose was named. John Cliffe, a zealous mountain climber of the 1840's, has described him for us, a type that survived to our own time. Scraggy, scrawny, and hardy, hatless and fired with the same fervour which exalted the troglodytes and stylites of the Arabian deserts on to their pinnacles, he pursued his religion in the insistent traversing of all the sky-line ridges of Snowdonia. How many of us can recall that fervid passion for following the 'true' ridge over all its obstructions! If we knew something more of this parson's ascents we might hail him as representative of the transition from scrambler to rock climber.

The attraction of mountains for the religious mind is apparent throughout our records. For some reason unexplained, the High Church bishops and deans sought out the lofty Alpine peaks, while the evangelicals and Dissenters congregated largely in our northern and western hills. From the first, clerics seem to have been almost in a majority among hill lovers. Besides those already cited, the Revs. George Freeman and John Parker had traversed Snowdonia during the first decades of the nineteenth century, and written of their adventures. The connection was never broken. In the 1880's I can remember a mild black-bearded minister, known to us as the Welsh Shepherd, who beckoned guests on arrival at Pen y Gwryd, quoting Kingsley's thunderous invitation to himself on his own first appearance there: 'Come inside, sir. We all sit in the bar, at Pen y Gwryd!' —a natural enough summons to modern ears, but almost scandalous to a Victorian, and as between parsons. A year or two later we spent a long day in cloud searching all round Cwm Glas for the reputed Parson's Nose; and the mists, opening a window below us, suddenly framed a rock profile projecting from the crag, an aquiline episcopal nose of the haughty Wellesley type. We never could find it again; but it seemed then as though Snowdon had been sealed mysteriously to holy orders.

2

Under the young and hospitable farmers Harry and Anne Owen, Pen y Gwryd had become, half-way through the century, a hill inn, which welcomed the coming of the hill explorers, the searchers for new impressions fortified by Ruskinism, the anglers intent on always higher tarns, and the returning Alpinists. It was these last who set the fashion of winter ascents, an improvement at least upon the night walks. Winter climbing was a reasonable first choice for those pioneers on Alpine snow and ice. During the summer our hills seemed too bland for their enterprise, since the possible all-the-year-round sensationalism of rock climbing had not yet been revealed. Harsh wintry weather, snow-filled gullies, and frosted precipices fed the new mountain passion almost as effectively as the glittering and equally foreign splendours of the Alps. The fireside warmth, hot farm food, and consoling drinks to be found at the valley-head inns provided an exotic contrast after the freezing returns from the summits; and they tempted further the bold assembling of parties of friends at Christmas or Easter, to celebrate sociably in British fashion the right opposites of hardship and compensating comfort.

Pen y Gwryd was ideally placed for the purpose, at the meeting-place of great valleys, on the watershed between great ranges, looking across the southern precipices of the Snowdon craters at Gallt y Wenalt, one of the finest buttresses of power in Europe and a rival to the great Zmutt ridge. P.Y.G. possessed all the potentialities which made Zermatt famous, except for any differences that may be detected between the seasonal magnificence of Snowdon and that of the Matterhorn.

Charles Edward Mathews, the Alpine pioneer, became a devotee of Snowdon and of the inn in the 1850's, and he has left us the story of the great men of his time who attended the assemblages at Pen y Gwryd. We owe it to these returning Alpinists that they formulated mountaineering as a creed rather than as a technique, and so began the chronicles of their mountain visits and of their colleagues as something worth recording for the future. In this way we learn of many distinguished but otherwise unrecorded friends of Snowdon in the past: famous names,

Coleridges, Gladstones, Lytteltons, Buxtons. Adams Reilly, 'one of the most gifted of men' and the cartographer of the Alps, and Frederick Morsehead, 'fleetest of foot of the Alpine brotherhood,' were among them. I remember seeing, in the bar, Morsehead's small jutting grey beard outlined against Mrs Owen's mob-cap, while his large fair son described his father's bold survey of the Lliwedd East Buttress, where then still only terror reigned.

Illustrious names these, that might well have obscured any lesser luminary. But there was a touch of eighteenth-century gorgeousness about Charles Mathews, an enlargement of well-lit and dramatized personality, that marked him out among his able midland and southern contemporaries, the business men and clerics who formed the select body of the pioneers. Circles crystallized round him, as clubs did about Cecil Slingsby. He founded the Society of the Welsh Rabbits, which used to meet in different Welsh centres, under himself, Hulton, or Horace Walker, for the purposes of winter climbing and sociability. To him too we owe the records of the Pen y Gwryd visitors' books, which later fell into disrepair during the years of the Owens' decline, and were first salvaged by Hugo Young, Q.C., and subsequently rebound in full by Charles Sayle, the devoted Cambridge librarian.

Winter climbing had its vogue. Huxley, Tyndall, and the first of the mountaineering Busks bought rake handles for fourpence in Capel Curig, turned them into alpenstocks, which were then *de rigueur* as aids to a descending balance, broke through the annual snow-cornice above the Wyddfa zigzags, and revelled in a view, as Tyndall describes it, of an orange magnificence equal to any splendour of the Alps. There is another description, too little known, written in the *Alpine Journal* by H. G. Willink the artist, of his winter climbing in 1878 on Snowdon and the Glyders. It brings to life the deep snows and the bitter cold of all winter climbing memories, the wind-blown icicles and the fairy-like frost-feathers on the summit transfused with gold light. Surprisingly, he conducted 'some conversation with the echoes of Clogwyn du'r Arddu'—prophetic echoes, perhaps, and of what future climbers calling? When his party tried a sitting glissade down a snowy couloir, and of course somersaulted, it was 'young

Harry Owen who showed the greatest amount of centrifugal eccentricity.' (See Plates 3(*a*) and 13(*b*).)

This winter climbing was already good mountaineering. The title scrambler was outmoded. Rock climbing had not yet achieved separatist recognition, but the word climber had come to stay. Cliffs and crags had begun to have an interest for themselves; the crude gullies on to Crib Goch found mention in inn books, and the Trinity gullies on Y Wyddfa had even a name. At what moment did rock climbing for its own sake become a conscious purpose? In Switzerland, in northern England, and in Wales the gully shadows under pent and pitch began to catch the mountaineer's roving eye, promising mysterious and dilatory but connected passages to a crest, and an emergence into sunlight or the comforts of the 'colde winde.' With the naturalness with which water flows into and down a channel, the early rock climber drifted into and up the inviting gully. At first this was because it held steep snow and offered an obvious exercise in Alpine snowcraft; but later it was because gullies had shape and identity and length without breadth, as lines of ascent, and they resembled one another instructively in their problems, of upright steps and helpfully contactable walls.

The gully epoch, as it was later identified in *Mountain Craft,* was launched by a gradual revelation. When in 1883 and 1884 Stocker, with Wall and then Parker, first climbed the Lliwedd precipices, a cliff had been climbed definitely for its own sake, and not merely as a route to a summit. This was the earlier of two distinct shifts of accent in the history of mountaineering which we have seen taking place during the last half-century—successive shifts of interest from the hill to the climber. This earlier shift we made almost unknowingly, when, in a period of transition, rock faces or ridges ceased to be incidents on our way to the summit, and became objects of our climbing day for their own sake. I can look back with surprise at a time when it would have seemed to me unworthy of a climbing day to fail to go on to the summit of the mountain upon which our rock climb had been made. The second change, when the interest shifted so completely from the hill to the climber that the mountain surface could be altered for his purposes, will be mentioned later.

As the nineteenth century closed, the sporadic parties of friends climbing from Pen y Gwryd were unconsciously accepting the first change of accent. They were changing from winter couloirs and iced ridge scrambling to steep rock gullies and the giving of names. The pleasure we take not only from pride in our own success, but from sharing that achievement with others—the prime mover in the development of all sports—was hard at work, multiplying the novices and the inquiring friends to be introduced to the new activity. But the Alpine revenants remained for a time the preponderant force, the nucleus round which were formed all early climbing clubs. In Wales Charles Mathews, Bryant the white-hooded eaglet of a secretary, the boisterous Nunky Halliday, and the reverend patriarch Nelson Burrows remained of the older tradition at Pen y Gwryd, with no thought of specialized rock practice. But W. E. Corlett, dark and restless, and his companion Marshall Smith, a Nansen-like figure whose deep voice and sincerity contributed much to our early traditions, knew that ice and snow work even upon Welsh cliffs needed an apprenticeship, and with the younger Hopkinsons, Sydney Donkin, and the Pagdens belonged to a transition period; while Tom and Roderick Williams in the Tryfan North Gully are credited with the first roped rock ascent in Wales.

The rope, we may recall, was only spasmodically used, here or there on a climb; and with something of the same apologetic manner that embarrassed the first hammerers of pegs into rocks. Old Alpine ropes and hay ropes and washing-lines, they were put on or taken off as casually as they had been by early Swiss guides. The connecting rope was not yet regarded as a continuous or even a respectable insurance policy; and it had no communicable technique, although books on sailing were searched lightheartedly for tips about knots. The accident to Evans on Lliwedd in the 1880's, one of our first strictly climbing accidents, which made a sensation at the time, was due to this casual usage.

Things had been moving faster in the north, with Slingsby, the Pilkingtons, and the Hopkinsons to lead the way. Haskett Smith, with his little red books, the first of all our home climbing guides, in mind, had raided west and south, and combed the Welsh ranges for the upright crags he preferred to all other

mountaineering.   Owen Glynn Jones, and his pupils the Abrahams, had followed, with the same purpose for larger volumes,
and had collected magisterial gully climbs.   When clubs and
their journals came in their order at the turn of the century, the
book of rock revelation was opened, betraying where the climbs
lay and something of their characteristics.   With that, history
and nomenclature and the rapturous vanity of recorded first
ascents, together with the rumours of unrecorded, *positively*
first ascents, all started up together.

The simplicity of the primitive attitude towards rock difficulty
made all the more daring, we may think, pioneer feats, such as the
botanist Bretland Farmer traversing the untrodden Lliwedd East
Buttress at mid height; or Stocker, and again Eckenstein, working
out lines up the abrupt West Buttress; or, shortly afterwards,
Archer Thomson's habit of contemplating and breaking through
successive 'impossibilities' up the frontal precipices; or again
A. W. Andrews's solitary and sturdy wanderings in rubbers and
audacity, high among the Lliwedd cracks and juts.   And it was
Andrews's diverting paper in the *Alpine Journal* which made the
break-through, for Welsh rock climbing, into the Alpine sacred
circle.

These were writings on the wall predicting change.   Others
had preceded them.   There was a sensation in the tranquil gully
years when J. M. A. T.'s small artistic script appeared, briefly
recording his ascent with Harold Hughes of Twll Du by cutting
up the frozen waterfall, a new departure on home hills.   I had
known another, when I was basing on Ogwen, and had spent the
day failing to scale the unclimbed rock wall of the Kitchen.   On
returning to the cottage I found two unknown young men, quiet
and insistent, W. R. Reade and W. P. McCulloch.   Two days later
news reached me that they had climbed the Kitchen on the day
after our talk.   Another writing, and on a notable wall.   As a
comment, I should add that these advances in skill have always
appeared to me to form a steady progression; they have been
advances that overlapped, owing to an improving adaptability.
There have not, in my opinion, been the sudden jumps, new
revelations, or startling miracles by the succeeding sons of the
prophets, which their admiring contemporaries have at times

2. George Borrow (1803–81).   (After the portrait by H. W. Phillips)

generously claimed for them. J. M. A. T.'s climbs, for example, reigned supreme, until all imperceptibly they were surpassed. Gibson's and Ward's direct ascent on Glyder Fach for a time represented the *ne plus ultra,* and then was merged. The haloes round Herford's climbs, particularly his and Sansom's Flake Crack, melted gently into the trajectory of new starry courses.

In the same transitional period, Oscar Eckenstein, an engineer, with the build and beard of our first ancestry, was, I believe, the first mountaineer in this or any country to begin discussing holds, and the balance upon them, in a theory with illustrations. He had moved up with Frederick Gardiner from Pen y Gwryd to a shack at Pen y Pass, which he had fetched out of the Snowdon mines, and as I watched him hanging ape-like from the rock face of his eponymous boulder below the wall, and then passed my hand between his lightly touching fingers and the rock, it was the first suggestion of the balance and foot climbing later analysed in *Mountain Craft.* Archer Thomson practised with him, trim and dark-clothed, with lion eyes and mane, and supple, silent movements. He became by a short head the first practising master of this conscious skill.

At the beginning both of the century and of the transition, the inn opened at Pen y Pass; and this led to a move, more or less purposeful, among the keener climbers, upward and that much nearer to Lliwedd and their cliff climbing. But climbing rocks must not be thought to have had then the connotations we now attach to the term rock climbing. To understand past history we have always, with difficulty, to put our minds back into a point of view no longer our own or that of our generation. Mountaineering had not then long been recognized as a sport or even given a name. The word climbing had not yet its specific meaning of a technique or skill. It is always hard to imagine that any popular activity ever could have had a beginning, especially so recent a beginning. I have seen the Guide to the Trinity Roofs referred to as though it had been only an episode in a long history of undergraduate roof climbing; whereas the conscious formulation was so entirely an innovation, that even the propriety or legality of such climbing had never received consideration by the authorities through all past centuries. Similarly, mountain climbing at the end of the last century still meant a new adventure, in unknown country and under strange conditions   It was an enterprise even to reach hills once or twice in the year; the cliffs still took finding; and the Climbers' Club could still declare a bold intention of fully exploring the Welsh mountains.   Rock climbs, also, were still regarded as existing lines of possibility contrived by Nature, and concealed for us to find.   They were our discoveries of Nature's already existing bounty, not inventions of our own.   It was a point of view very different from the modern conception of a climb, as a line of all but impossibility, to be forced anywhere and everywhere, by skill or mechanical ingenuity, up and over every natural obstruction.

We have to keep it in mind, or better in imagination, that mountain climbing still meant going up mountains, and that rocks and cliffs were only incidents on the way.   Crags on lower slopes and foot-hills did not come into question as a true day's climbing. The boulder practice such as we obtained on rocks near our base, on off or wet days, was a limited exercise which could do little to improve the technique of the time.   It was not until the climbing infection spread over areas without hills, where the solitary out-crop of gritstone or sandstone played the part of the local moun-tain, as it did in the Peak District, that bouldering, as we called it, could come into its own as practice on a large scale, and produce its experts.   Herford and Laycock were original and conspicuous examples of a truth which only became recognized fifty years later, that practice and a progressive training on relatively low and technically difficult rocks of this character are the essential pre-paration for attempting modern severe rock problems.

It would be an anachronism to assume that during these early years any 'schools' of climbing, a Lakes school or a Welsh school, could have existed.   There were few climbers, and most of them went as much to Wales as to the Lakes, and only less often to Scotland because of the long journey.   Each climber went on his own, with a friend or two, and rarely met other climbers.   The few books or guide-books that began to appear could have as little effect as other climbers, while style was still unconscious and individual.   O. G. Jones's writing, for instance, helped greatly to make climbing known; but his own method belonged if anything to the forceful style of the gully epoch, while George Abraham, who learned from him, was already a foot-and-balance climber.

While the change in stress was proceeding, Pen y Gwryd, having survived a post-Owen period of courting the tourist from afar with kid gloves, had kept its proportion of the faithful, even after the passing of the pioneers and the exodus of the rock men. It had been the birthplace of the Climbers' Club at the turn of the century, and it retained its friends and its traditions. Tryfan and the ramifications of Lliwedd West Buttress were darkened with the long and leisurely ropes of the capital M's: Moss, and Marler, who was club treasurer for eleven years and in office for seventeen; S. Marples, librarian for sixteen years and in office for twenty-six; Mordey, small and as ageless as Bryant or Time; Morrish, an original member. Then the Gotches, father and son; T. K. Rose, another original, Alfred Ewing, wittiest of officials; the L's: Lowen and Lehmann, for so long a key mountaineer; the Nettletons, a notable pair on many athletic fields, and Mrs Nettleton, one of the first supple movers on slabs.

Names from an earlier era were still to be found among the visiting groups. Neat-bearded Bowring, reputed to have climbed every mountain in the island; wild-bearded Dakyns, to whom his colleague T. E. Brown wrote the noble *Three Places, Dakyns!* and whom we used to meet, still emerging out of the mists in Cwm Glas, his continual resort of geological study; literary figures, the Havergals, Augustine Birrell, the two Kingsleys, Arthur Godley and his inseparable companion George Wherry, the surgeon and *littérateur*. Myles Mathews, as secretary of the Climbers' Club, unweariedly carried his father's foundation through the years of weakness that accompanied the social and economic changes produced by the First World War, and he succeeded to his presidency. A big man of many talents, he was the mainspring of the club, introducing activities, constitutional crises, a reformed journal, pocket guides, and his own writing. No loss was sadder for us than his early death, followed by that of his gay and gallant son Guy in the Second World War, the last of the dynasty.

A faithful group continued with him, and after him, at Pen y Gwryd; and a remarkable feature of their climbing may be noted

here in anticipation.   Contented as Pen y Gwryd had been to
trek comfortably up Trinity or Tryfan gullies, or later to disen-
tangle the maze of routes on Lliwedd West Buttress, the First
World War produced a noteworthy effect upon the standard of its
skill and the scale of its undertakings.   The veteran climbers
emerged from it in a very different class.   The reputations of
Robertson Lamb, C. W. Marshall, M. G. Bradley, J. M. Davidson,
B. K. O'Malley, even of C. F. Holland, were deservedly made
after the First World War.   Meanwhile A. E. Elias, E. S. Rey-
nolds, and R. Williams are figures associated with the beginnings
of the new Pen y Pass movement, led by Archer Thomson; and
he was joined later by A. W. Andrews, Professor Orton the bird
and weather expert, Leonard Noon, and Humphrey Owen Jones.
They were in the process of learning to stand on tiny ledges and
one nail, and had forsaken for ever the imperative footsbreadth
which had compelled the Alpine pioneers to prefer snow or ice
to rock, because an adequate width of tread could always be
fashioned there.

3

All of us who had moved up to Pen y Pass were soon in full cry
after the new doctrine of climbing.   We began to generalize
from our common knowledge of a series of local climbs.   Discussions in the smoking-room intruded upon lighter evenings;
and here Leslie Shadbolt, Archer Thomson, H. V. Reade, W. R.
Reade, Humphrey Owen Jones, Geoffrey Bartrum, and a little
later Claude Elliott, Harold Porter, Hugh Pope, David Pye,
Trev. Huxley, Conor O'Brien, Mallory, and Herford took active
part.

If it may seem to the modern climber that rock skill developed
only lazily at the turn of the century, after its recognition as a
sport, the reason still lay in the difficulty of reaching cliffs often, or
quickly enough to secure more than a few days or hours of
uncertain weather, for sustained practice.   Only a localized
climber such as J. M. A. T. could become familiar with the cwms
and their crags; or at best a mercurial Mallory might race over the

Photo by R. Williams

3(*a*). Pen y Gwryd in 1892

Photo by B. R. Goodfellow

3(*b*). Pen y Pass in 1939

ranges for the chance of finding a good crag, and return after nightfall. Foot's-pace carts were slower than tramping. The normal climber, untrained, made for the nearest or well-known cliffs, where he could be sure of a climb even in bad weather, and of finding the way home. To reach the tops of mountains was still the underlying aim of the day. Eminent crags could capture attention; but they did so better when they lay on the line of the mountain ascent. Dinas Mot, for instance, fitted upon the shoulder of Crib Goch, and its profile was early explored. When 'Bishop' Evans and I made the ascent of the Dodo Gully on Craig Cwm Beudy Mawr, it was the more satisfying because this cliff also was moulded upon the configuration of Crib Goch. Pope's Sylph Route on Lliwedd, a day he spent alone in ascending and descending all the best pitches of the East Buttress, and Herford's Ogwen exploits on lower crags, called for all the more amused attention because they were marked exceptions. I have even a dim memory of taking part in craggy explorations on Craig yr Cwm Du, where the open fretwork slabs were spread so thinly upon the heather that it was breaking through the holes we used for hands and feet. These were experiments, in a new type of calculated climbing for its own sake, and they were taking place simultaneously in Switzerland, and on crags such as Kern Knotts in the Lakes.

Of the new figures associated with this phase and the beginnings of Pen y Pass, W. R. Reade has perhaps not received the credit due to him, and which his self-effacement avoided. His was a steady influence, bridging the generations and the years. Lean and bony and hard-featured, with a short crop of greying hair and a smile that warmed the heart, he had much of Franz Lochmatter in his make-up: the same short body and long steely legs tapering to small feet, the same tentacular movement on rock, with the same composure and tranquil independence of others. He was only interested in new climbs: Jordan on the Pillar, the Central Cracks on Lliwedd, the outside route on Crib Goch pinnacle, with a mute preference for disappearing down the Llanberis Pass with anyone he could persuade to join him in explorations on the Columnar crags.[1] As often happens with his

[1] Dinas Cromlech (Plate 8).

D

type of mountaineer, probably a good deal that he did went unrecorded because he felt it to be incomplete. Geoffrey Bartrum had joined him, and shared in many of his pioneer climbs. While Reade's unobtrusive influence did much, both before and after the First World War, to advance younger climbers in Liverpool and the north, Bartrum, through the years and the Second World War, acted as genial counsellor in the south to generations of our climbing clubs, encouraging a succession of younger administrators, whose influence has extended over the mountain world. Theirs was a long partnership, of imperturbable good humour. I realized it first when I watched them from the Lliwedd Bowling-green, worming up the slabs below, by what is now called Reade's Crack. It happened that Conor O'Brien and I twice worked out new routes, one up these slabs and another up the outside of the Crib Goch pinnacle, only to find that the pair had been before us, and that we had made two more of what Archer Thomson called 'second first ascents'!

All first-rate climbers have styles of their own; and their climbs now began to reflect the different styles. Andrews rubberroamed, goat-like, up ribs; while Bretland Farmer followed or preceded him with the sinuous slither, and something of the look, of a seal at the zoo. Herbert V. Reade, cultivated and precise in aquiline profile and exact movement, tiptoed lightly upward. His long feet and short stature enabled him, it was said, to take a toehold and lean forward in balance between himself and the rock face. I saw him blown off the ledge ahead of me by a high wind, as we walked round Cwm Glas; he alighted on his feet below, and walked on undisturbed. H. O. Jones, another short and weightless figure, climbed with a smooth flicker, which agreed curiously with the inward fiery spirit on which he achieved his mountaineering eminence in the Alps. Archer Thomson, as he climbed or leaned back in survey, looked in closer touch with the crags than with his companions; centaur-like he seemed to belong to the rocks he bestrode, and to be moving gently in rhythm with them. Probably climbing styles were more diverse while they remained still unstudied and unconscious. George Mallory's I have elsewhere described. He swung up rock with a long thigh, a lifted knee, and a ripple of irresistible movement. A perfect physique and a pursuing mind came together as it were in a single-ness of power, as he rushed into motion.   The little Irishman Edward Evans, who often climbed with him from Pen y Pass, contrasted amusingly.   Red-haired, a fine horseman, and emotional under the alternating obsessions of the Gaelic move-ment and orthodox Anglicanism, he was known as the Bishop and climbed with a startled petulance.   That fluctuating mood we saw again in Ivan Waller's tidal perfection upon rock.   Evans and Mallory, after J. M. A. T. had returned from his Great Chimney with a grave but flowery description that no one liked to challenge, went up to climb it; and failing to identify it from the account, scaled the open slabs beside it, now called the Wrong Chimney, because, they protested, they 'looked quite as much like a chimney'!   C. G. Crawford was silently effective and adroit on similar exposed slabs.   David Pye and Ralph Todhunter were compact and elegant climbers, with initiative.   Pye led on climbs such as the first exploration initiated by W. R. Reade in Cwm Silyn, together with Porter and Claude Elliott.   Todhunter undertook with Mallory the writing of a guide to the outlying cliffs beyond the Snowdon area, as soon as cars had made these reasonable.   Conor O'Brien, another of the Irish contingent, a short sturdy blue-water seaman of a dozen talents and skills, treated rocks like rigging, climbing barefoot, with a pipe alight and an unbroken flow of comment, apostrophe, and philosophy. His first-rate books of voyages have also a mountaineering interest, and his romances for boys contain impeccable sailing and rock climbing.   Harold Porter, long-bodied and prehensile, with adroit hands for many skills, led brilliantly when in his best form. He wrote the additional Ogwen guide for us; but his greater mountaineering was in New Zealand, where, introducing cram-pons, he set a new standard of difficult ice and snow work.

Leslie Shadbolt was another of our swift and agile climbers, of independent mind, in search of new cliffs and new regions. Raymond Bicknell was a master of the skills of the period, almost handicapped by size but equally great in enterprise.   Both have left their mark on the history of British mountaineering.   George Macaulay Trevelyan, upon racing feet, swooped like an eagle above every hill region, and wrestled up wet Welsh gullies and over snow-covered Snowdon ridges: so enchanted by the world of severe open-air beauty that he devoted the half of life and fortune to the safeguarding of these historic scenes and our fells. A. M. Mackay, ablest of early Scottish climbers and of venerated law-lords, shared our rock explorations in wintry Wales, before shifting to the Alps and to rock pioneering in his native Scotland.

Siegfried Herford (Plate 4(*b*)) had something of a Norse wind-god in his fairness and sudden apparitions on high, unlikely pinnacles. He was an originator; but his first wish was admiringly to repeat all Pope's climbs. His lead up the Flake Crack on Scafell, undertaken for a climbers' guide to the Lake climbs similar to our Welsh guide, which I had arranged with the Oxford Press, is sometimes cited as the beginning of the transition to modern methods and standards. It is probably the first recorded use of slings or stirrups as aids since Alexander the Great. An engineer, with a deep strain of poetry and romance, his style of rock climbing would have been at home among recent developments. From his knee to his shoulder there looked to be a single powerful spiral of muscle, which enabled him to straighten in balance upon infinitesimal stances.

Most good rock climbers, not excluding the greater stars in the present firmament, would seem to belong to this type of well-sprung figure of medium height, with a long reach. The ideal climber approaches more and more nearly to his forest prototypes. In the zoo as a boy I watched spellbound the agile gibbon swinging from point to point with incomparable grace. His only rival in movement has seemed to me the Italian puppet Bil-Bal-Bul, inimitable in his abandon, undulating on his trapeze passionately and bonelessly through space to celestial heights. These are ideals still left for future climbers to realize.

The big men, of the long stride and reach, come into their own again in general mountaineering. Hugh Rose Pope was a superb example. Six foot four in statuesque height and an all-round athlete, he climbed with an indolent but fluent certainty and balance, and with an advantage of reach that devoured rock distances. He, if anyone, might have led the new phase in mountaineering, as mature and masterly in his Alpine and rock feats as in his writing. I made a chance selection, in the Pen y

Pass hall one night, of a dawn rescue party for Pen y Gwryd climbers benighted on Tryfan North Buttress. All were over six feet: Raymond Bicknell, George Ingle Finch, Hugh Pope, Trev. Huxley, Nigel Madan, and was it Claude Elliott or Julian from Ireland? Seven finer all-round mountaineers could not have been found in the world at that time.

The Etonian group had early become prominent. Charles Donald Robertson, Trevenen and Julian Huxley, Nigel and Geoffrey Madan, Hugh Pope, Nigel Finlay, Claude Elliott, Norman Young, and, independently, Marcus Heywood, Strickland-Constable, and Ferdinand Speyer. Under the Harrovian inspiration of Arnold Lunn a number of them produced the *Oxford Mountaineering Essays*, a unique contribution to mountain literature, and they created the Oxford Mountaineering Club. The revival of the Cambridge club after the war was, in similar manner, due to Claude Elliott. Their social contribution of impromptu songs, essays, and games to our climbing company made our mountain evenings memorable.

There was an elastic number of Irish climbers, who sailed over in O'Brien's yacht: versatile artists, lecturers, architects, and musicians, with Page Dickinson as graceful leader. Inspired by Wales, they initiated the exploration of the Irish cliffs half a century before the Irish Mountaineering Club was formed, and they were great promoters of the Gaelic literary movement. I have explained elsewhere why I discouraged the poet Yeats from coming climbing with them. Their gaiety, songs, repartee, and witty commentary on all our climbing incidents survive in memory, and they form a happy contrast to the gloomy overtones of strain which depress so many later stories of mountain acrobatics.

There were other contingents, some of earlier date. J. Osborne Walker and C. H. Hadfield brought parties, in the classic style; George Morse joined us with his boys, renewing his climbing youth; Cecil Slingsby and his family; the George Gasks, sage and strenuous. Akin to Morse, the hereditary mountaineering Pasteurs, Willses, Nortons, and Carslakes, Letts and the soldierly Carfrae brothers, formed separate elements of good looks and distinction.

Pen y Pass expanded its shacks, and its welcome, to hold us all. The Harry Owens had provided the right contrasting atmosphere of warmth and light in the wilderness; and the Rawson Owens and Miss Jones, arriving at the right moment, renewed the cordial Welsh tradition. Owen's car succeeded his dashing brake and pair; private cars multiplied, and climbers extended their range of cliffs accordingly. On the windy pass, and almost by chance, we anticipated the luxury of later climbers' huts, with electric light and the best of all bath systems, sitz-baths close round a blazing stove, with shouts through rain and storm producing relays of hot water from an exclusive outdoor cistern. We remember best in contrasts. Unforgettable are the endless discussions of details of climbs from bath tub to tub; with Frank Smythe, perhaps, crooning on his mouth-organ, perched in a bath towel on the back of the bench; Tony Smyth, the notable airman, and Humphrey Trevelyan, now the Ambassador to Egypt, or O'Brien and Longland, in abstract argument through the steam; and George Mallory or young George Trevelyan leaping to do slow circles over the roof-beam—until a blast of hail and protest let in the hot buckets and the boots together. On the blaze followed the black contrast of the beat across to the hotel against driving sleet and gale, with the sense of great mountains and grey crags rising through darkness and mist behind the wind; and the burst of coloured lights as the hall door clanged open, upon the glow and welcome of the crowded dinner company, with its indulgent evening of songs and laughter and often ingenious fun.

I need not hesitate to recall the social and personal aspect of these primitive years. While climbers were slowly and unconsciously developing novel ideas of balance and adhesiveness hitherto only the secret of circus and gymnasium, their sociability in face of the mountain opposition and the original quality of much of their writing and speaking also did their part: they helped to spread knowledge of the mountains and, in the end, to accelerate the coming of climbing skill.

In a spirited movement to further the cause, and the new club, it was arranged that leading climbers should each take over a number of the *Climber's Club Journal*. The numbers produced by Myles Mathews, George Mallory, Arnold Lunn, and Trev.

Huxley especially, were successful in establishing a high literary standard during the experimental years when climbing was still regarded with suspicion, and some hostility, by the lay public. Together with Percy Farrar's good work as long-time editor. of the *Alpine Journal*, these first efforts in English climbing journalism maintained the reputation gained for overseas mountaineering by Leslie Stephen, Whymper, and the writers in *Peaks, Passes, and Glaciers*. A tradition was established which our climbing journals have done everything to support and confirm.

It has no importance for our climbing record, but it says something perhaps for the calibre of the men first attracted by the romance of the hills, and of pioneer climbing, that of those who came on Pen y Pass parties, as I look through the list of names, three earned the Order of Merit, four had the Nobel Prize, five became Cabinet ministers, seven were made peers and one a life peer, fifteen were knighted, and of course an indefinite number became honorary doctors.

The amateur spirit, as it might be regarded now, presided; much the same amateur spirit which animated our soldiers and officers, until the terrible losses of the First World War enforced a more professional teaching and attitude. Courage was all. Charles Donald Robertson, of heroic mould and by reputation the ablest man in the Civil Service, was killed in attempting to climb up to his limit on Glyder Fach, untrained, on the first morning of a mountain holiday. In memory of a great mountaineer and mountain writer, the chapel and monument were erected at Glansevern within sight of the mountain, and the Charles Donald Robertson Trust was created, to take Cambridge undergraduates to the hills. This, one of the first beneficial endowments established without other test than personal impression and record, was reproduced in the Irvine Fund at Oxford; and it has later been copied in principle and on a far greater scale by the Swiss Mountain Foundation and the Everest Foundation.

This tragedy threw a shadow upon the joyous adventure of our own mountains. Until then the dramatic threat of great height and depth, of the frail balance and the breathless hand-cling, had had an atmosphere of unreality, like the danger of a dream from which we feel we shall wake.　Probably even now many climbers, with all experience and history to learn from, never really believe that they can fall, or suffer from the effects—until they have done so.

Mountain ascents still formed the foreground of our climbing; and hill walkers and scramblers of the older fashion still belonged to our company.　It was expected of all gifted climbers that they should devote some part of their holiday to securing others' pleasure, and it might always happen that a clumsy but distinguished elder was in search of a new sensation, or a boy or girl in need of introduction to rock.　This altruistic convention put a certain restraint on the best climbers.　But if it was a check upon skill, it was not felt in a period when those by nature prehensile represented the highest development in climbing skill, and further progress entered into no one's mind.　To the dignified judgment of early mountaineers the caricaturist Samivel's humorous nightmares, his out-of-balance convolutions in webs of attachment to rock ceilings and vaultings, seemed diverting fantasies, but that they could ever be realized by human beings no one would have been foolish enough to imagine.

Other climbing clubs were by now struggling into existence, started by encouraging elder Alpinists.　A more localized younger generation was beginning to learn its business by trial and error, in the then few holiday seasons.　The Rucksack Club, for instance, trained upon the Milestone Buttress above the Holyhead road, educating in this sound fashion the remarkable group of climbers who took the lead after the war.

But it is illustrative of our steady change of view, or of stress, that this was also a buttress at which I never thought of glancing in those years; it lay so far below even the terrace from which we started our Tryfan climbs.　Of the bouldering order of climbing, it did not then seem to deserve the whole of one of our few mountain days.　The introductory gully and the primitive crack up the Idwal Slabs were regarded in the same light, as moist and arbitrary starts for the genuine climbs upon the higher Glyder faces.

In the first years of the century, after the tentative starts of these few older climbing clubs, I remember making inquiries at both Cambridge and Oxford, as to whether a climbing organization for undergraduates would find any support.   Especially were we interested to discover whether a branch of the existing Climbers' Club might find favour at Cambridge, if Charles Sayle and a few others initiated it.   But we had to give up the idea.   The Alps were still the goal of the few younger folk who had the mountain feeling; and for an undergraduate Alpine Club there was then, of course, too little chance of getting experience, and the journey was still too costly.   The idea that mountaineering could be developed up to an Alpine or expert level on our own hills had as yet taken no hold.   It was not until 1906 that W. Calvert, the son of the genial Yorkshire mountaineer, called us in to support his launching of a Cambridge club from a Trinity nucleus; and in 1909 it took the dynamic personality of Arnold Lunn, with such climbers as Pope, Huxley, Madan, and Bourdillon, to do the same for Oxford.

But in the few years preceding the First World War, so gifted seemed that younger generation, like a flowering of the race, as it came in always increasing numbers to join our small band of climbing enthusiasts, that it appears now as we look back to have been a Golden Age.   The war came; and it eliminated much of the more leisured class, and destroyed the balance between work and cultivated leisure.   It altered the conditions of mountaineering no less than all our other circumstances, and it shuffled the social elements from which climbers were drawn.

4

After the war, climbing clubs that were based only upon big towns, with no local root among hills, suffered most.   The luxury of two or more social clubs was impossible, and any social organization had to offer concrete advantages to be worth affording.   But what was lost by the clubs was gained in part elsewhere.   The romantic aura surviving from the days of mountain exploration had died with the disappearance of the generations that had leisure for adventure and for the coloured presentation of life.   But an intensified study of practical skills and profitable sciences could now extend its grasp so as to embrace also rock climbing. Young men hardened by years of military training, inured to a common hardship and danger, released at both ends of the social scale from any social order and all former prejudices about clothing, open-air sports, bathing, and risk, were eager for the excitement and chances of the cliffs.

The lower and more accessible Welsh crags, often the more weather- and water-worn and therefore suitably small-holded, began to be sought out and presented as practice grounds in technique. Idwal Slabs, again as an example, were explored for new and increasingly difficult lines, and climbers were now even observed to be going up these and down again, without continuing appropriately to the summit of the mountain. I. A. Richards and Dorothy Pilley, by their ascents soon after the war upon the steeper and higher slab walls, did their best to restore something of the character of mountain climbs to these ventures. In any case, it was not until the Second World War, and the evolution of Commando training out of mountain experience and technique, that the rock practice and parade grounds were invented, and that Idwal joined the Cornish cliffs and other convenient crags as a crowded and jostling gymnasium.

The aeroplane following on the motor-car had by this time extended our climbing range. The Himalaya and further regions came within holiday reach; and the war aftermath sent restless minds mountaineering further and further afield. The older universities, which twenty years before could not digest a climbing club, were now mature enough for guideless Alpine expeditions. The ascent by Van Noorden and Wyn Harris, both notable Welsh leaders, of the Brouillard ridge on Mont Blanc was the finest performance of its period in the Alps. Financially, however, new Alpine activities were handicapped. The tradition of the amateur skills had been lost, and the guides to help in recovering them could not now be afforded by the young. Meanwhile the war had spread climbing like wildfire through the continental countries bordering on the Alps, which climbers from these countries began at long last to frequent in week-end fashion similar to our growing habit with our own hills. For the time being we could not compete with the Continent in new

Alpine feats; and this encouraged a mistaken notion that we had fallen behind in mountaineering as a whole, and that our home climbing was negligible.

In fact I believe our climbing, technically speaking, to have been improving at the same quickening pace as in any continental country. The Mancunian climbers had grown up, and Fred Pigott, Morley Wood, Eversden and their contemporaries had broken the spell which had kept cliffs of the standard of Clogwyn du'r Arddu inviolate. Simultaneously, Cambridge University produced one of its tidal waves of mountaineering, in a generation that has provided many rock experts and many great mountaineers: among them Van Noorden, Wyn Harris, Gino Watkins, Noel Odell, Jack Longland, Ivan Waller, Freddie Spencer Chapman, Basil Goodfellow, Tom Brocklebank, Charles Warren, Robert Chew, Humphrey Trevelyan, the three Bicknells of the second generation, the two Wagers and two Wakefields, Ted Hicks, Bryan Donkin, Peter Lloyd, E. A. M. Wedderburn, and Michael Gordon of Slingsby's third generation.[1]

The Pen y Gwryd elders, as already noted, rose with the war to a new standard; and C. F. Holland, C. W. Marshall, and M. G. Bradley led a series of advances. Oxford responded to Cambridge with fewer numbers, but with fine quality: Douglas Busk, W. M. Younger, Herbert Carr, Raymond Greene, and Maurice Guinness met the efforts of the Climbers' Club to reinforce itself by an increased university connection, with an energy which still reverberates. Raymond Greene went on to lead the scientific thought on Himalayan exploration, and Herbert Carr stayed, to break down old barriers of time and space, and range widely through the Snowdon cwms and up innumerable crags, supplied by the shepherds with appropriately Welsh Welsh names.

The name of Creigiau Gleision on Foel Goch returns in this context to mind, as an instance of how far remoteness had protected all outlying regions in pre-car, pre-war, pre-Carr days. The novelty of this fresh discovery was no doubt magnified in J. M. A. T.'s romantic mind by the fact that, in 1910, even for him new cliffs were growing scarce and shy. For an excited spell the

---

[1] Philip, of the fourth mountaineering generation, is already climbing in the Pass.

tales of it loomed large, very much as had the first stories of Avalanche Route and Great Chimney on Lliwedd under the same magnifying glass. The ridge of Creigiau Gleision lost its lustre and became a mirage in a single evening of tropical smoking-room discussion, when the noted geologist Fearnside protested: 'You couldn't find your Great Arête when the grass is long!' and: 'What there is will crumble to dust where anyone treads heavily.' He was right, in so far that it had vanished from mention by 1920 and the coming of the new climbing intake.

Remembering the restrictions upon our climbing time and space before the war, I am surprised not so much by the slowness as by the smoothness and precision with which the interest in rock and the capacity to scale progressively severer angles on it developed. But the losses among leading climbers in Wales had been, and continued to be, heavy, even apart from the war casualties. C. D. Robertson, Stoop, and Salt had fallen in 1910, J. M. A. T. died suddenly in 1911, H. O. Jones and Pope were killed in 1912, Herford fell in the war. Soon Mallory was to disappear on Everest, Marshall was killed, and later both Raymond Bicknell and Todhunter fell in the Alps. The serene Victorian tradition died hard, that life was sacred and better stored in a napkin, and youth a suspect state to be repressed, safeguarded, and ordered for its ultimate issue into manhood's dangerous currents. In the illogical fashion peculiar to our countrymen, this had been combined dangerously with a sense of personal dignity which permitted no stooping of the head under fire[1] or betrayal of awareness of danger on a precipice. The margin of safety allowed in climbing under these conditions, which was first defined in *Mountain Craft,* was a vague and neutral area, previously undefined by any exact technique, and subject to emotional alterations, but by now hardening to definite and narrower limits.

Even so there was a slight pause after the war in new Welsh enterprise. Our old routes were again grassed in and mossed over, and had to be refound. The rush of reaction filled the hills with a crowd of assorted ages and interests, famous scientists

[1] Herford died through raising his head in a trench—not necessarily an accident.

and uprooted citizens, from whom for the time being climbers emerged with difficulty. Then the new climbing names began to appear; and simultaneously new Welsh cliffs seemed to click into focus, recorded by Herbert Carr's and G. A. Lister's fresh enthusiasm. As already indicated, the broad signal of the change was the progressive move on to Clogwyn du'r Arddu, up till then very wisely left alone to its echoes of Willink's voices. Frank Smythe, just out of the Air Force, was on fire for its exploration. Pigott and Morley Wood, penetrators of the East Buttress, courteously waited to share the first ascent of the West with him and the Cambridge climbers. I lay watching the ascent from the little tarn below, in sunshine, and I began then to realize how far climbing had moved forward in those gradual years and in the war interval, very much as a glance at the clock face can tell us from time to time how far, and how imperceptibly, the hands have travelled.

From the foot's-breadth of hold to the nail-hold, the margin of safety had invisibly contracted. Skill was becoming an end in itself. The Idwal Slabs of our disregard were now, like the Napes Needle, providing an ideal theatre for the appraisement of style, and our elder surviving climbers were here joining the younger entry in displaying their new progress. It was from below the Slabs that I had another glimpse of the hands of the clock almost as they moved. The big New Englander Colman S. Williams, whose energy had been flung into almost all Cambridge activity but who had never climbed, surprisingly became visible, travelling up the leaning vastness of the Slabs from the far right-hand corner, on soft soles and finger touches, slanting upward across all vertical known routes to the left-hand sky-line, then back across and up, to the terrace under Holly-tree Wall. Shouts alone diverted him from the overhang; and he careered downward and about the Slabs, ending in a run down the steep start of Hope, with a sitting fall in the little swamp at the finish, which rubbed in a needed moral. The mean angle is no more than forty-five degrees; but it was a demonstration suggesting a new departure, and the prospect that the rhythm which we had set as a remote ideal that might be attained by continuity in movement, could in fact be realized in ordinary practice.

I have always watched rhythmic movement for pleasure; and in studying and practising climbing movement I had come to the conclusion that, if climbing were ever to make any further progress as a skill, there must be continuity of movement even on difficult rock. The 'cling and kick' of the gully era had quickly given place to balance and footwork. But we must not stay content with the 'stop and restart,' the staccato style of this second phase. In the further past, when I was writing about the right but neglected method of climbing down, I had advised the 'touch-and-go' or 'rimless wheel' movement; but our skill was then still too undeveloped to contemplate such continuity, or rhythm, on severe upward climbing. However, soon after the war I was invited to watch C. D. Frankland on his Almscliff verticals and overhangs, and I had the satisfaction of seeing him illustrate fully for the first time continuous movement up severe rock, with its rhythmic fluctuations and grace.

As yet another effect of the post-war economic change, the shift of centre from the hill inn to the climbers' hut came almost unnoticeably, but as definitely as the shift in mountaineering accent. Ogwen Cottage had at an early stage supplemented Pen y Gwryd and Pen y Pass as a convenient base for the cliffs, with Snowdon Ranger for a time as outpost. A few farms had opened their doors. But after the war, and Helyg,[1] came the deluge of club huts and youth hostels, for the most part adapting with some taste the existing venerable buildings to hold the new vintage of cragsmen. Pen y Gwryd revived, to the lasting benefit of the faithful; and for a time, as a tribute to tradition, oncoming climbers spared a few days and evenings to share the social parties at Pen y Pass; while their now far-flung week-ends were devoted to a new seriousness at Helyg and other club bases as they were opened. War had left its permanent aftermath, and not least in a liking for organized activities and specialization. The nineteenth-century individualism, part of the disappearing Liberal tradition, was gone, and with it went the exclusive type of

---

[1] The derelict cottage by the Holyhead road, which Borrow had referred to as a 'wretched hovel,' was opened on 30th October 1925. It had then a single room measuring 15 by 20 feet. Primus burners were used and water carried. It has been greatly enlarged and electricity installed. See page 65 for its present condition.

mountaineer who had declined joining any club, even the classic
Alpine, lest his communion with the mountains might be diluted;
and who only shared a few evenings of sociability at Pen y Pass
with anxious reservations as to the independence of his mountaineering day.

Herbert Carr's achievement, in establishing Helyg as a Welsh
home for the Climbers' Club, not only ended our club-caravan-
ning through the London wilderness, but provided an invaluable
nursery for rock climbing as a skill for its own sake.   W. R.
Reade, Geoffrey Bartrum, and Sydney Donkin saw to its comfortable installation; and from it Marshall, Mackenna, and then
Stuart Chantrell encouraged or chastened the flying feet or too
aspiring spirits of the new school.   There was no break with
good tradition.   Much of the best of the old was passed on, with
just the shift of accent in the direction of technical skill which had
been made inevitable by the disappearance of much of the
unknown, the incalculable, and the romantic from our home
mountaineering.   There had to be a fresh stimulus to adventure.

5

The changes in our home conditions were all in favour of the
rock climber rather than the mountaineer.   Easy approach to the
hills made frequent visits possible.   Frequentation produced
familiarity with height, depth, and angle; and to this that constant
human agency, acquired adaptability, was actively contributing.
Each generation of climbers seemed to acquire more readily,
almost atmospherically it might be thought, the co-ordination of
eye, judgment, and corresponding movement which their predecessors evolved only through laborious years.   The formulation
of a few simple climbing principles was by now preventing
the worst of our primitive errors, the nervous and instinctive
hand-clutch and haul, and the concave body-cling to the rock.
Climbers, too, were now drawn from an always widening field.
They had ceased to be an intimate and selective group, of the few
falling under the spell of the mountains or in search of unknown

adventure.   As the rumour of rock climbing spread it attracted the games-player, the physical hazard-lover, the open-air gymnast.   Leaders of climbing ropes on difficult cliffs had no longer to be picked out conscientiously each day from among the few born climbers.   They multiplied out of this new wide intake, by training, example, and infectious adaptability, until they had become, no longer the exceptions, but the majority in any mountain assembly.

The shift of accent, and of altering skill, became all the more noticeable if ever greater mountaineers visited our hills during and after the time of change.   When the great Captain Farrar rock-climbed, it was on the traditional high-mountaineering and massive method, with rich abuse for undue rock obstruction. The famous Dr Blodig, in our earliest period, came to climb on the same ample lines.   But by the time the post-war French experts, Henry de Ségogne, Paul Chevalier and their colleagues, paid Wales a welcome visit, it was rock, the hardest rock problems and competitive rock for them, all the way and all the day. Later again, the Munich climbers had the same rapacious eye for the vertical, and they first introduced Wales to pegs as adventitious aids upon it.

From every quarter, between the wars, experts multiplied rapidly.   H. M. Kelly, G. G. Macphee, Alf Bridge, Alan Hargreaves, and, later, men such as Tony Smyth the airman, F. R. Dodd, and K. Tarbuck—these picked up the older tradition with fluent adaptability and had soon intensified its practical application.   Climbers still felt they belonged to every hill region.   But among those supposedly of northern bias were George Bower, A. T. Hargreaves, and Sid Cross.   Maurice Linnell's amazing ascents had already had something fatalistic in their character, and splendid young Dick Barry fell later in South Africa.   Indeed mountaineering continued to exact an always heavier toll for its great adventure, in the lives of some of the very ablest and finest: John Hoyland, Nully Kretschmer, John Jenkins, William Bell the young poet, and the irreplaceable organizing mountaineer and comrade, John Barford.

The Cambridge group of this date has been mentioned; with whose primacy had soon to be classed the feats of Wilfrid Noyce.

Photo by A. W. Andrews

4(*a*) *(above)*. Pen y Pass Group, 1907.

Standing: O. K. Williamson, ———?, Marcus Heywood, G. Winthrop Young, J. Percy Farrar, J. M. Archer Thomson

Seated (middle): W. R. Reade, Geoffrey Bartrum, George Mallory

Seated (front): E. B. Harris, F. Don, F. Sparrow, Oscar Eckenstein

4(*b*) *(right)*. Siegfried Herford climbing. *See* page 38

Oxford responded with John Hoyland, Robin Hodgkin, David Cox, John Ryle, Warr, and two of the climbing Viney brothers; later, with Mervyn Hughes. Clubs multiplied through all universities. The excellent institution of small splinter clubs formed among a set of friends and contemporaries took root in the towns, supplementing the large climbing associations. They revived something of the personal intimacy of early climbing groups, which were reluctant to share their mountain days with any but those of a like outlook. As soon as the idea had been accepted that climbing was a technical skill which could be mastered, and therefore taught, it was conceded that boys and girls could be included in the mountaineering fold, with proper safeguards. Mountain clubs began to form even in the schools: Harrow, with its exploratory Marmots, and Marlborough with some great future climbers and a journal printed by the boys. The typescript climbing records produced by the small boys of the Birley Senior School have always seemed to me one of the most praiseworthy of all mountain literary efforts. The Scouts had begun to encourage a mountain section; and a correspondence which Baden-Powell maintained with me over a number of years shows interestingly the gradual change of attitude towards the dangers of the sport taking place in the views of organizers and parents, as public opinion about mountain climbing altered with the wars, and with the passing of the age of security.

The same continuous development was to be observed in the mountaineering of women and girls, as they joined us in Wales. Little time seemed to have passed since the darker ages when a cousin, Edith Stopford, in a pioneer climb on Lliwedd, had impatiently torn off a foot's-breadth of Irish frieze skirt to be free for a foothold, and it had lain through long seasons on the East Buttress as a touch of colour and of protest against a perishing fashion. But by now the triune personality of Cottie Sandars, Maryanne O'Malley, and Ann Bridge, a born mountaineer, could stride up the crags in less hampered movement. Another author and hereditary climber joined in, Katharine Hopkinson, with Theo Chorley; others included Ursula Nettleship; Hester Pinsent, with E. D. Adrian; Virginia Kennedy, with David Pye; Mabel Northcote, with Arnold Lunn; and Ruth Mallory, with

E

George, and later with their brilliant climbing daughters Clare and Beridge. Eleanor Slingsby, with her brother Laurence, had led the Tryfan buttresses before the war change. Bronwen Jones, sister of H. O. J., had been the first to demonstrate how much more adept girls were at climbing on the first slab discoveries than at wrestling up throttled gullies. And now, after the war, Brenda Ritchie emphasized the advance; and unforgettable in Cwm Silyn was the sight of her light movement in leading a rope of men up the great slabs.

It was again after the First World War that the admirable climber Mrs Kelly founded the Pinnacle Club, accepting my suggestion of the name, so that girls' skill, and their credit for it, might be independent of masculine muscularity. Eleanor carried on a Slingsby tradition by becoming the first president of a new club. The Pinnacle Club, appropriately, was founded at Pen y Gwryd, with Lilian Bray, Mrs Eden Smith, the Wells sisters, Dr Corbett, and Mrs Daniells (E. H. Young the author) assisting. So far has the change gone that we now see on the crags women professionally instructing boys and men.

The acceptance of the fact that skill in climbing could be taught brought with it, but very slowly, the further recognition that the effects of a mountain training upon character were capable of definition, and therefore of transmission. We had begun the discovery by realizing that climbing could do boys and girls no harm; but we were still some way from understanding that the inspiration and discipline from which we had profited much ourselves in mature years might be good for them also. It took the imagination of a great educator, Kurt Hahn, and the emergency pressure of the Second World War, to formulate methods which would make use of the direct educational influences to be found in the adventure and in the service of the mountains and of the sea, now combined in the Outward Bound Movement.

The pointer towards change swung slowly further. The experiences learned in war as to appropriate kit for rude conditions brought about a marked change in climbing garments and outfit. The changes favoured skill and balance. The heavy corduroys, boots armoured like battleships, columnar stockings with capitals, leather reinforcements, capes, gaiters, helmets, weighty ropes, and ponderous sacks made up a heavy handicap. Saturated with rain and all the water of the Welsh hills, the weight used to be doubled. After the usual wet days the drying-rooms roared and steamed all night, and the shrunken, damp, but scorched resumptions in the morning were grim struggles. The Laocoön coils of our thick soaked ropes felt leaden upon the shoulder; and indeed I wonder how any leader ever surmounted a delicate passage in balance. The change had now come, and once again unremarked.

6

In every branch of art or science it is from the progressive collaboration of eager minds in competition that the outstanding genius or leader emerges. Mountaineering is no exception. In the few intervening years before the Second World War the culmination of free rock climbing was reached; and it was typified in the series of ascents made by Colin Kirkus and Menlove Edwards (Plate 5). Kirkus's style was not unlike Herford's to watch, but substituted a slow adhesive trimness for power in balance. The movement agreed well with his neat figure, close wavy crop, and large tranquil eyes. On any new attempt he moved gradually, steady in his readjustments, and reassuringly. In contrast Menlove Edwards, brown-locked, full-limbed, and amber-tinted, moved as dynamically and sinuously as a glittering anaconda up any graceless vertical, preferably a corner dripping and forbidding. They were both artists in the craft, and both were writers, with a breath of romance about their often solitary achievements. With them it almost seemed that the hands of the clock had gone full circle, returning upon the era of the first amateur Welsh adventurers.

I use the word 'free' climbing of climbing done permissibly with aids that may help the personal security, such as waist-rope, nails, rubbers, crampons or axes, all of them safeguards attached to the climber; but done without direct modifications of the rock or mountain surface, such as fixed pegs and their elaborate extensions in slings and stirrups and pulleys. It used to puzzle me in the past to find any point at which the introduction of artificial aids must stop, because each one led logically to the next. And yet, if no limit were to be accepted, climbing it was plain must end up in sheer mechanical apparatus and aerial suspension. But I believe now that we can, and certainly should, draw our imaginary line between alterations to the person of the moving climber and modifications of the permanent surface of the rock or mountain. Continuous contact with the natural mountain surface should be the final criterion of 'mountaineering' proper. All other exercises upon prepared surfaces may well pass as just 'climbing.'

The debate amusingly begun by Morley Wood, when he carried up stones in his pocket on Clogwyn du'r Arddu, to jam as a belay in the crack from which the essential pebble had fallen, seemed at the time to have ended in a joke, when we decided that a stone native to the cliff might be thus restored, but not an off-cumden imported. But in fact we may now see the jammed stone as the thin end of a prodigious wedge, embodying an altera-tion not natural to the mountain and predicating immediately the metal peg, the hammer, and the pulley.

The distinction between 'mountaineering' and just 'climbing' lies upon this line; and it should be made clear in the terms we use. Especially should we make it clear among the present-day armies of beginners who know only the wayside crag at the week-end, and believe that to be the end-all of mountaineering. Indeed, the crag-sport has become so popular that at times in this mechanical-minded age greater mountaineering and its chronicles are spoken of as if they were an eccentric and archaic branch of the New Rock Climbing. This is not said in disparagement of crag climbing. On the contrary, if our increasing numbers of climbers are to be free to indulge their own passion for novel and greater feats, then the multiplication of these slings and pitons for challenging fortune are in a wholesome line of succession, exercises excellent for health and recreation. All experience, even of mechanical contrivances, is an arch through which gleams some untravelled world. But such climbing should not be called mountaineering: it demands a different type of nerve, of skill, and above all of judg-ment; and it is far more limited and material in its object, as also in its effect upon character, upon thought, and upon inspiration.

5(*a*). Menlove Edwards

5(*b*). Colin Kirkus

An absorption of mountaineering by rock climbing, of the greater good by the lesser, is the second of the two changes or shifts of accent which, as I mentioned earlier, have been prominent in the development of our home climbing. The shift of interest from the mountain to the climber, from the adventure to the skill, threatens to become all too complete. In the growing emphasis we place upon the pleasures of self-realization, even our Welsh mountains, their greatness and adventure, are vanishing in the background, behind the assertive brilliance of the climbing hero's halo. If we did not foresee this, we have at least been long aware of a gradually altered lighting. We know how much of our own delight was drawn from the remoteness and silence of the cwms and hidden cliffs, their uncertainties and sudden surprises out of the unknown, and we resisted guide-books for as long as was reasonable. Especially did we fight to delay the graded lists, which under headings such as Moderate and Severe, descending later to bald numbers, seemed to classify rock acrobatics technically above great mountaineering routes, and by their concession to human vanity, the flattery of being able to skim off the cream-climbs that head a list, can beguile young climbers on to the valley-side boulders, in the fond belief that these represent the greatness of mountaineering.

As long ago as soon after the First World War some effects of this shift of interest began to appear; and I recall speaking to the Oxford University Mountaineering Club on the subject. They were moved to pass a resolution renouncing the use of all guide-books and written descriptions, so that their pristine mystery might be restored to the hills and cliffs. A heroic resolve, and worthy of the Oxford past; but I fear that it too joined the lost causes.

The Second World War has served to intensify the change of view. Rock climbing became the chief Commando activity and method of training; and with the emergency usage came the licence to use every expedient in the attainment of its objectives. Highly specialized instruction in every detail of climbing technique has remained available after the war for the youth of every city and every kind, and this at the age most adaptable and pliable for mastering a physical skill. It is often schoolboys now, as we may read, who have become the customary leaders of their elders (and of one another) upon the most audacious climbs.

Rock climbers can now be grown upon every crag. No one would wish to reverse the order of progress. But greater individual and racial benefit is to be had from greater mountaineering; and we should do well to attempt to preserve the distinction, between a wholesome rock activity and real mountaineering, even among our own hills. The attraction of the great mountain explorations opening out in the Himalaya and further ranges will help to emphasize our meaning in making such a distinction. We should also, and for much the same reason, avoid making comparison between climbers, or their standards of achievement, in the succeeding phases of our history in Wales; when it was more important for the survival of our pioneers, and for our climbing future, that they should make progress in the elements of mountaineering and the degrees of mountain danger than grapple with gravity on overhangs. Each phase in Wales has had its experts and its own upper climbing limit. In each phase there has been much the same distance between the experts and the average climbers of the day. And each phase, with improved training, practice, knowledge, and apparatus, has merged unnoticeably upward into the next; and the new generation has made new valuations by an improved general standard.

Mountains must always remain the largest objects of beauty in our country, in their nobility of line, in their seasonal change of lovely colour, and in their severity of wind and weather chance. Unless men become brain-pods, with utility tentacles controlling machines through a monotony of space, there will always be climbers to whom the Welsh wayside cliff and 'the creste of the cragge' will bring the exultation of physical prowess and health, and—whether they seek it or not—the knowledge of themselves; and there will always be a proportion of men and women born with the feeling for mountains and the comfort of 'the colde winde,' for whom Snowdon, its ridges, precipices, lakes, and shadowed valleys, will hold open the gateway to adventure.

III

The Greased Pole
A survey of rock climbing in Wales since 1927

by

GEOFFREY SUTTON

The Greased Pole

I

IT is easy to write objectively of remote events, and personal reminiscences retain something of the freshness of contact, but events that came just before an author's own time are bound to be for him a sort of no man's land between past and present; they affect him intimately though he had no part in them. For this reason I have drawn largely on the work of others for the first part of this chapter, especially that of the late Nully Kretschmer,[1] making however such changes of emphasis as my different perspective would suggest.

The modern era of rock climbing in Wales seems to me to have begun with Fred Pigott's ascent of the East Buttress of Clogwyn du'r Arddu in 1927. This climb surpassed by far anything that Wales had seen up to that time for sustained difficulty and seriousness, and gave Snowdonia its first rival to the great routes of Pillar Rock and Scafell in the Lake District. Between 1918 and 1927 Welsh climbing had carried on the unhurried tenor of pre-catastrophic days, the tradition was still Pen y Pass and brass bedsteads, Lliwedd and Ogwen; a leisured, cultured atmosphere still untroubled by presaging ripples of the storm that was brewing farther north in the Lakes, where the pushing urban spirit of this century was driving restless young people from the northern towns up ever steeper, longer, and more difficult mountain walls. Writing of this period in Wales, J. L. Longland has said:

The last four or five years of the 1920's may seem an odd period to choose to write about, neither post-war nor pre-war, a little late for Herbert Carr's revival of the [Climbers'] Club and a bit earlier than the greatest days of Kirkus and Edwards; a fluid sort of time in which it was still not yet clear whether the mainspring and centre of the Club's most active climbers would still be Geoffrey Winthrop Young's

[1] 'Rock Climbing between the Wars,' *The Mountains of Snowdonia*, 2nd ed.

parties at Pen y Pass or the small and doubtful new venture at Helyg
. . . by the end of the five years about which I am writing the hut had
succeeded the mountain hotel and the week-end teams were more
numerous than the sociable Easter and Christmas parties, and whereas
Carr can still refer in the Helyg log-book in 1926 to Beddgelert as Club
Headquarters, by 1930 Helyg was the unquestioned centre of the Club's
activities.   In recording something of these changes, perspective can
best be kept if one begins with a quick backward glance.   The making
of the good roads, Capel Curig–Bangor and later Capel–Llanberis, in
the early years of the nineteenth century, the acquired mountain habits
of 'the literary, the learned, and the artistic elements,' the discovery that
British hills gave good practice for more serious Alpine seasons,
gradually brought into existence Pen y Pass, Pen y Gwryd, and Ogwen
Cottage, which were the cradle of Welsh climbing tradition and in
time of the infant Climbers' Club.   Undergraduates, dons, and schoolmasters turned mountain reading parties into climbing parties, and
before the turn of the century C. E. Mathews and others like him had
founded the type of party, regularly meeting each year at P y G and
composed of Alpine Club friends, which for years to come was to be
responsible for exploring the possibilities of Welsh climbing.   So our
Club came into being, founded by frequenters of P y G with C. E.
Mathews as its first president, and although in the early 1900's the focus
shifted to Pen y Pass and leadership passed for twenty years to Geoffrey
Young, the method and the tradition remained substantially the same.
The regular Christmas and Easter parties changed in composition,
included women, bridged three generations at once, and gave far more
care to the training of beginners, but they remained companies of
friends and of the friends of friends, and, as Geoffrey Young makes
clear in his chapter in *The Mountains of Snowdonia*, they came together
as much for sociable as for mountaineering ends, and were valued for
their contribution to the 'good society' more than for their eminence
in the distant world or even their prowess as mountaineers.   We
nevertheless owe to them our present technique and the whole set of
our climbing habits, and modern climbing is explicable only in terms
of the discoveries of the innovators in their ranks, Eckenstein, Archer
Thomson, Geoffrey Young, A. W. Andrews, W. R. Reade, and later
on Mallory and Herford and Hugh Pope.   'The slab and face ascents
which are now the main feature of our rock climbing were the invention
of these new masters; and they were only rendered possible by their
patient and ingenious elaboration of novel balance style. . . .'   To sum
up, from 1919 to about 1925 Welsh climbing showed no new inventions

of importance. The first great period of exploration, sustained at a high level for many years, seemed to have petered out, and losses caused by the war had been heavy. By 1925 H. R. C. Carr had completed his intensely valuable work of publishing the results, up till then available only in the Pen y Pass book or in the folklore records of the original explorers, of the climbing accomplished to that date on all the crags in a wide circle round Snowdon which had not been included in Archer Thomson's two books. . . . By 1925 it had become clear that the standard of new invention and technical achievement was for the time being much higher in the Lake District than in Wales, and that the Welsh pioneers had not yet been succeeded by climbers of comparable stature. The Club itself, started by C. E. Mathews and his friends [in 1898], invigorated later by new recruits and by its lion's share in the discovery of new climbs, both stemming from the central impulse of the Pen y Pass gatherings, was now again after the war in the doldrums, with no continuous home in Wales and no fixed headquarters in London or any other district. With public transport improving, and cars just beginning to come within the reach of modest incomes, the number of regularly visiting climbers was rising, but it was still quite uncertain whether the next forward movement in exploration would come from members of the established seasonal parties or from those who were catching the week-end habit. Meanwhile, the general level of performance was not high, and the abler climbers were, if young, finding their way on the classic routes, and, if older, mainly content to repeat what they had done before the war. . . . So 1925–30 appear now as preparatory years, years in which the balance was shifting from one type of Welsh climber to a new kind . . . in which some of us had the rare privilege of being admitted to the fellowship of two different climbing generations, who nevertheless, for all their differences in achievement, understood and liked each other well.

A quotation from Geoffrey Young himself may serve to complete this backward glance:

The heyday of the small mountain hotels, in their happy solitude at the remote end of long walks and slow cart-drives, is probably over. Quick, motor transport, the changes in the economic and social order, and the coming of the hostel, the climbing hut, and the camp, have accompanied the extension of the mountain enthusiasm to every class and occupation, with different ideals of sociability. Mountain hotels in their survival are likely in the future to be only a small part in a more general provision; and they may have to provide for less romantic and cultivated, if more material and exacting, demands, than in the days when only the literary, the learned, and the artistic elements thought their remote simplicity worth while.

This tradition, vital and manly in its prime, the years before 1914, seems in retrospect stagnant in the years following the world upheaval, and eventually the charmed web was bound to be shaken and then shattered by the ruder, but refreshing, gusts of a new age. The mountain inn, as it is referred to in the foregoing paragraph, may well serve as a symbol of the whole world of mountaineering in our time. The changes and developments which it is my task to sketch in this chapter must be seen and understood against the back-cloth of more general history— the booms and slumps of the age of mass production, the background of industrial ugliness, the spread of education and ideals of democracy uncritically accepted, the eventual redistribution of wealth. The difference between two climbs such as Avalanche on Lliwedd and Llithrig on Clogwyn du'r Arddu is the difference between Mr Owen's horse-drawn carriage in which, if he did not walk, Archer Thomson perhaps came to the hills that time, and the modern twin-cylinder motor-cycle on which Brown probably arrived : each an excellent achievement of the human mind, each fundamentally to the same purpose, but representing a different ideal or stage in a development which now seems inevitable, each one the creature of its time. And just as the Austin Seven or eight-litre Bentley of 1927 is closer in spirit to the car or motor-cycle of to-day than to Mr Owen's equipage, Pigott's climb was closer to our kind than to what had gone before.

2

It may be interesting to consider what, more immediately, brought these changes to Snowdonia, and how they came about. Transport we have already mentioned, and it played an almost incalculable part in the development of climbing. Whereas in the old days a climber from London or Leeds or even Liverpool might be lucky to reach Snowdon more than two or three times a

Photo by B. Hilton-Jones

Photo by W. Noyce

year, and then only by love and determination, it became possible
in the twenties for him to do so every week-end; though to begin
with it was only the north-countrymen who took advantage of
the fact.   Up to 1927 it was, as we have seen, mainly climbers
from the older universities and schools who, in their lengthy
vacations, made the technical advances in Wales, which came at
an appropriately leisured pace.   From this time forward, however, the varsity men even at their best could rarely hope to equal
the sustained virtuosity of those who visited the hills each week-
end, and whose evenings and off days out of season might be
spent on the small steep moorland edges of Derbyshire, Yorkshire,
and other counties.   Longland has summarized the matter thus:

Helped by long holidays, borrowed cars, and the fact that few tutors
refused exeats for short term-time dashes, we found ourselves often in
Wales or Cumberland for a day or two at a time, and so could get more
British climbing in the year than most of our predecessors managed in
their longer but more leisurely visits.   But we never came near to the
habit of coming to Helyg week-end after week-end, from Liverpool or
Cheshire or Caernarvon, and could not, as others later did, work away
steadily at a crag or a single problem.   Nor do I think we had
developed the mental attitude, as we certainly had not the technique,
that carried Colin Kirkus and Menlove Edwards on their triumphant
waves of discovery.   Our main planning and our pipe-dream ambitions
went towards each new Alpine season, or more distant ploys in the
Arctic or elsewhere.

The mental attitude is of paramount importance in difficult
rock climbing, and, as a great leader has remarked, most of the
gymnastics required are mental, but the vital confidence is closely
allied to physical condition, technique, and nervous habituation.

These things the new week-end climbers began to acquire by a
regular frequentation of the moorland edges just referred to.   It
would be hard to overestimate the effect that these gritstone
outcrops have had on the standard of climbing both at the top and
bottom ends of the scale.   The smooth rounded character of the
rock enforces a good technique, and the relatively low heights
make it possible for men to discover and extend their limits by
driving themselves to a degree not psychologically possible nor
very wise on the larger mountain precipices.   From 1927 to the

present day nobody has made an important advance on the standard of climbing who has not trained himself by regular outcrop climbing, and it is significant of the properties of grit-stone, if of nothing else, that every one of these pioneers has been a city-dweller from the towns of the gritstone area.

The purely social traditions of the older clubs found themselves somewhat alien to this new practical atmosphere. People were beginning to wonder if they served any good purpose at all and they were beginning to die from a sort of anaemia caused by the impossibility of renewing their blue blood, when they were given a swift and effective transfusion by the introduction of the club hut. Before 1914,

a club . . . meant something different from what it does now. Its intention and conduct were social, and it could only come into being around a nucleus of men of a certain standing, age, and fixed habitat, with the will and leisure to promote and to attend comfortable meetings and meals. The modern club formed by any mixture of dispersed younger folk to provide material opportunities, information, transport, lodging, is very different (Geoffrey Winthrop Young).

What was needed in 1925 was just such a mixture to provide just these material opportunities, and after a certain amount of hesitation the clubs set about transforming themselves. It is true that the Rucksack Club had tried out the hut idea before the war without success, but this was in rather an unfavourable place. In 1925 the enthusiasm and foresight of Herbert Carr and a few others caused the Climbers' Club to purchase a derelict cottage by the Holyhead road which George Borrow, long before, had already referred to as a 'wretched hovel.' Kretschmer has it that

at the time of its opening on 30th October 1925, Helyg was a cottage in which a single room of about fifteen feet by twenty feet combined the functions of kitchen, living-room, and dormitory, with some additional sleeping accommodation in the loft space under the roof. Primus burners were used for cooking and the soft twilight of a spirit lamp obscured the squalor of the scene. Water had to be carried.

The scene was set for the coming of the giants. At school we had a song with the chorus:

> For all of we, whoever we be,
> Come short of the giants of old, you see.

This is rather how one feels in writing about the heroic age of Helyg. This twilight of the climbing gods was at first presided over by the efficient but somewhat ferocious and dictatorial presence of C. W. Marshall. After his tragic death at Helsby in 1928, Stuart Chantrell was asked to take over the custodianship temporarily. Temporarily is a very elastic word, for E. S. C. is still benignly supervising the enlarged and improved Helyg we know to-day. Kretschmer goes on:

In 1927, the Rucksack Club acquired a farm cottage nearby at Tal y Braich Uchaf . . . it never experienced the boon of electricity, and possibly because of the resulting obscurity, members of the Rucksack Club have tended to pride themselves on the greater cleanliness of their headquarters as compared with those of the Climbers' Club. During the last war the lease of Tal y Braich could not be renewed and it was sad that the Rucksack Club should have to lose a hut with so many years' association . . . the Pinnacle Club acquired a cottage in Cwm Dyli in commemoration of their founder Pat Kelly, wife of H. M. Kelly the pioneer of Lakeland rock climbs, who lost her life in 1923 on Tryfan. The Midland Association of Mountaineers . . . bought the 'chalet residence' which stands on the shore of Llyn Ogwen, even if it does not exactly adorn it, and in this large house they provide more ample and luxurious accommodation for their members than does any other climbing club in Wales.

And the list goes on: the climbing hut had become an institution. About this time the youth hostels also began to bring increasing numbers of young people to the hills, but the most active climbers have always found their way into the clubs, and the club huts quickly became and remained, at least until very recently, the main bases of exploration. No one would recognize Helyg to-day from the description given above, with its bright paint, several rooms, library, ghost, and electrical appliances, and there is even a form of religious faith abroad that one day the chimney will stop smoking. The bath, too, is a highly efficient instrument of torture. Being square, it forces one to sit bolt upright, and as it is supplied by a completely inadequate hot-water cistern the hopeful newcomer is left shivering in a chilly three-inch puddle of water. At present only Thomas in the Climbers' Club is of sufficient stature to fill it by displacement. Similar blessings can be enjoyed at the Climbers' Club hut at Ynys Ettws in the Llanberis Pass, and at the Rucksack Club hut at Beudy Mawr in the same valley: and the innumerable other huts owned by these and smaller clubs all over Wales are only slightly less luxurious, which may account for the rumour that climbers seldom wash.

About the same time as his backing of the Helyg project, Herbert Carr performed another action full of influences for the future: he brought out his guide-book to Snowdon, which was the latest in the series of guide-books published by the Climbers' Club at the instigation of Geoffrey Young and others. Earlier volumes, on Ogwen and Lliwedd, had been written by J. M. Archer Thomson and A. W. Andrews and H. E. L. Porter, but the area dealt with by Carr was less explored, and contained far greater possibilities for the future, than these others. In particular it contained the then almost totally untouched Llanberis cliffs, and above all Clogwyn du'r Arddu, perhaps all in all the greatest cliff in Britain. The climbing history of the period 1927–56, which I am about to describe, exactly parallels the history of this cliff. Carr, who was among the first to attack its outlying buttresses, and who was himself of the opinion that the main buttresses could be climbed, was persuaded by others into making the following statements in the guide-book:

The great defects of the cliff are . . . the extreme steepness and north aspect renders it cold and repellent in any but the best weather, and even in summer it hardly gets any sun, except late in the day. . . . No breach seems either possible or desirable along the whole extent of the W. Buttress, though there is the faintest of faint hopes for a human fly rather towards its left side. . . . The scenery here is not surpassed on any crag in Wales. . . . The E. Buttress has never been climbed. The final wall is quite impossible, but the lower two hundred feet below a broad green gallery may yet be conquered by a bold and expert party.

As Menlove Edwards later put it, literature was adding her strongest inducements. The first to be induced were two Manchester climbers, Fred Pigott and Morley Wood. These two had climbed much on gritstone, and had perfected their technique in

Photo by J. Gianelli

7(*b*). The Devil's Kitchen: The traverse

Photo by J. R. Edwards

7(*a*). Lliwedd and Llyn Llydaw

the Lake District, where, as we have already had occasion to remark, the best climbs and the best climbers were at that time in advance of their Welsh counterparts. Even so they found the East Buttress of Cloggy a tough nut, and it was not until after several attempts by themselves and others that they succeeded. They chose what appears to be the easiest line up the buttress, though subsequent experience has shown it to be perhaps the hardest and one of the finest of those done before 1951—though such distinctions are hard to draw on this cliff where all climbs are great. It is however the best protected and least exposed. The route follows a series of walls and ledges and corner cracks, presenting gritstone-like problems, but with the qualifications of seriousness and scale. At that time it was probably one of the two finest in Britain, its only rival Siegfried Herford's incredible 1914 lead of the Central Buttress of Scafell in Cumberland. Perhaps the finest part of Pigott's deed was the overcoming of the mental barrier, for (in addition to its traditional inaccessibility) Cloggy, with its blackness, dankness, sheerness, and terrible unbroken bulk, is the prototype 'tall cliff, that rears its awful form.' Even to-day, when almost every corner and cranny has yielded up its secret, it is impossible to approach the cliff on a gloomy day without a contraction of the heart and a feeling of disbelief, a sense of treading on forbidden ground, as it lowers its massive denial over the llyn.

These great Rucksack Club climbers were presently joined by another group. And here for a time I do not feel I can improve on the words of Kretschmer:

Geoffrey Winthrop Young was living in Cambridge in those days. His influence, combined with that of the Climbers' Club and Helyg, directed the attention of a particularly brilliant generation of Cambridge mountaineers to North Wales. The flourishing of the Cambridge club, coming on top of Pigott's exploits, gave a great impulse to Welsh rock climbing. Van Noorden, whose tragic death in Cwm Glas in 1925 cut short a career that promised brilliance, ushered in this heyday of Cambridge mountaineering. . . . Ivan Waller was another . . . he climbed on Tryfan to the accompaniment of music from a gramophone. With its spectacular steepness, Belle Vue Bastion on the Terrace Wall of Tryfan seems typical of his genius as a climber.

F

Waller's contribution should be emphasized.   Longland has it that

Waller, having fortified himself by running up and down the Javelin alone, climbed Belle Vue Bastion on Tryfan with Stuart Palmer—a superb and Ivan-ish climb with, as Marshall put it, 'an agonizing step in it.'   A little later Waller climbed the Fallen Block on Crib y Ddysgl, and he has not perhaps been given sufficient credit for providing this foretaste of the harder short climbs which were to be done by Ted Hicks and Colin Kirkus a year or two later.

Kretschmer:

Many of the pioneering climbers of this generation were keen motorists . . . trained in this school of fast driving and hard climbing was Jack Longland, who became one of the great Cambridge leaders. With his scientific technique, Jack Longland was the first to complete a route up the West Buttress of Clogwyn du'r Arddu.   This was a great event, representing a combined effort of Longland and Pigott, with Morley Wood, W. Eversden, and Frank Smythe following.

The character of the West Buttress is different from that of the East.   Where the East is vertical and bald, presenting a great wall split here and there by deep-cut perpendicular cracks which make for a strenuous technique of climbing, the West shows instead a series of overlapping slabs, at a high but not vertical angle, which have been given a tilt to the left.   The climbing is thus more open and delicate, and the climber habitually finds himself either poised in balance on small holds in a position of delectable exposure, or pulling over the overhang formed by one of the overlaps.   Longland's climb presents both these character-istics, and once again the psychological feat was fully equal to the physical one.   'One advanced a foot or two at a time, digging for holds and removing turf piecemeal, yet the rock beneath was sound. . . .'   Like Pigott and Waller, Longland is a man of medium height and lithe, compact build.   A forceful personality, he was above all a technician and a balance climber on rock, qualities which speeded his development into one of the best British mountaineers in the Alps and elsewhere. Kretschmer again :

The exploration of . . . [Clogwyn du'r Arddu] . . . with its singular climbing difficulties set the standard for the new climbs, and its opening up by the routes of Pigott and Longland began a new golden age of Welsh climbing.

1928 was a bad summer but 1929 was exceptionally dry and fine. During September of the same year Ted Hicks, climbing in the Oxford bell-bottoms fashionable at the time flapping loose around his ankles [*sic*], had a remarkable fortnight.   He pioneered the East Wall of the Idwal Slabs by finding routes up the steep bubbly rock of Ash-Tree Wall and Heather Wall.   He climbed the Rowan-Tree Slabs and made a girdle traverse of the Holly-Tree Wall.   Among his other efforts there is included the direct start of Longland's climb on du'r Arddu, up the steep, wet, loose rocks which are so much better avoided.

This Cambridge group was joined by Alan Hargreaves and, rather later, by Alf Bridge.   These two climbers fulfilled a special function in providing a link between the great pioneers and the other climbers. They were present on many first ascents, and often one of them was responsible for the second ascent of one of the great new routes.   Alan Hargreaves climbed much with Colin Kirkus and also with Menlove Edwards.   Alf Bridge was often the companion of that very brilliant leader, Maurice Linnell, who so tragically lost his life on Ben Nevis in 1934.

Hargreaves is a small, light, wiry type of climber.   Bridge is burly and of great strength.   On one occasion in the Lake District he was leading the great flake pitch of Scafell Central Buttress without combined tactics at the chock-stone (which had not been done at that time), and as he was laybacking up the final section his foot slipped off the wall.   As he fell he reached out and caught the chock-stone with his left hand—and held himself. Few would be capable of such a feat.   It may be added that he finished the climb—but in the conventional manner!

Kretschmer goes on:

And now the stage was set for the appearance of Colin Kirkus. This quiet, rather queer-looking lad, when taken up by Hicks's Cambridge party to Glyder Fach, amazed them by pointing out a steep right-angled groove which merged into an overhanging crack, as something he thought he would like to try.   This was considerably steeper and more lacking in large holds than anything which it was customary to climb at that time.   He promptly climbed Lot's Groove on a rope and then repeated it as an unaided lead, only Hicks being able to follow.

The next day he led the shorter and even more difficult Central Route on the Terrace Wall of Tryfan and this time none of the Cambridge party was able to follow.

To a later generation Lot's Groove seems perhaps slightly the harder of these two climbs, and Hicks's Rowan-tree Slabs perhaps harder than either. They were none the less outstanding achievements. Kirkus was nineteen years old at the time, and had the faculty of early daring and confidence which is characteristic of those who make the great advances in rock climbing. To their own (or rather their contemporary) generation they are apt to seem crazy, but their own generation is in reality a generation which they create, and which follows long after.

In the following year he [Kirkus] found the Great Slab route on the West Buttress of Clogwyn du'r Arddu. With no knowledge of what difficulties lay in the six hundred feet above, this tremendously exposed climb required mountaineering skill of the highest order. In technical difficulty . . . the Great Slab now ranks below a number of other climbs, but it will always remain a considerable undertaking for any climbing party, and at the time of its discovery was an outstanding mountaineering achievement.

This very balanced assessment by Kretschmer states the case exactly, and I am at a loss to see how anyone can justify the statement (which has frequently been made) that this was the boldest lead ever on British rock. It is difficult to make out in what way it was bolder than some of Herford's; or Longland's lead of his climb; or Kirkus's own solo first ascent of the equally exposed Pinnacle Wall of Craig yr Ysfa; or several subsequent performances by others, each in its time.

In the same year he found his Direct Route up the nose of Dinas Mot, a perfect climb in its steepness of clean rock, and with the delicate balanced movement which is needed to surmount its difficulties. Colin Kirkus excelled at all types of rock climbing, the open slab requiring delicate skill, as well as the steep chimney requiring tenacious strength and endurance. There was nothing showy about his climbing, in fact he took things slowly and was occasionally awkward and ungainly in his movements. He was not temperamental and never got rattled even under the most difficult circumstances. Under a diffident exterior was hidden a great driving force. He was not merely a gymnast, though he was a brilliant technician, but also a wonderful route-finder and above all a man endowed with rare qualities of endurance and energy, and an engaging facility for eating a large meal at any time.

Chantrell records that:

Those of us who made regular visits to Helyg will never forget the sight of his sitting at the table on a Sunday evening polishing off everything left uneaten. He might commence with a tin of bully, go on to a large plate of porridge, liberally spread with syrup and butter, and then proceed to clear the table systematically. It was a most impressive spectacle.

Kretschmer continues:

Before the war he was in business in Liverpool. He was a navigator in the Royal Air Force when he lost his life in action over Germany.

His first ascents on the East Buttress of Clogwyn du'r Arddu of the Chimney Route, of the Curving Crack, of the Birthday Crack, and of the Pedestal Crack—the most strenuous of them all—bear testimony to his versatility and enterprise. They are all hard climbs on steep rock, requiring much courage and strength. On the first ascent of the Chimney Route, Edwards was second man.

It was no coincidence that both Edwards and Kirkus came from Liverpool. Only climbers living within easy reach of the Welsh hills could take part in the intensive development of that period. Liverpool is only seventy miles from the Nant Ffrancon valley, and it has a convenient training area in the [sandstone] outcrop of Helsby Rock, where both Kirkus and Edwards had climbed much.... Edwards, like Kirkus, is a man of middle height, but where Kirkus appeared almost slight in build, Edwards gives the impression of tremendous strength which is by no means misleading. Above all, strength characterizes his climbing. There have been occasions when he chose and conquered the Open Slab, but it is in grasping the Great Overhang with his main strength and struggling with it hour upon hour that he stands out most. He does not always struggle. Sometimes he simply dissolves the difficulties and appears at the top of his cliff as if by magic, but mostly he struggles and wrestles and labours, but with what effect! There is an entry in the log-book at Helyg in which he describes nineteen routes for ascending the little boulder in the Helyg grounds. This includes every possible way, every permutation by which any more or less normal human being could possibly ascend this rock. This painstaking thoroughness is typical of the man.

The exploration of the cliffs of the Devil's Kitchen in 1932 and 1933 was the first of the consolidated efforts which are so typical of his climbing career. He extended the diabolical domain with Rocks, Buttresses, Pastures, Dumps, and Dives. With occasional excursions to the upper cliff of Glyder Fawr some fifteen routes on the Kitchen cliff were pioneered by him. Most of them are severe in standard, all of them are in places which are steep and dark and which were, at any rate at the time of discovery, overgrown with vegetation and buried under loose rocks.

By inclination Edwards confined his climbing to cliffs near to his base at Helyg, and always to parts which were new. He added routes on the Milestone Buttress of Tryfan, on the Terrace Wall, and on Gallt yr Ogof.

It is a curious fact that almost everything that Colin Kirkus touched became climbing gold. He moved sporadically from cliff to cliff, and wherever he went he unerringly picked out a few of the great routes, then moved on. His climbs are characteristically clean, sound, exposed, in fine position, and often feature long unprotected run-outs. They have architecture: they were this quiet man's means of self-expression. He developed early and almost all his great discoveries were made in the few years between 1929 and 1934, when he was involved in the accident that caused the death of his friend and only peer Maurice Linnell. This incident profoundly modified his attitude to climbing, and ended his exploratory period in Wales. His Alpine record was curiously undistinguished, but he showed his accustomed brilliance in the Himalaya and might, but for prejudice in certain quarters, have taken part in pre-war Everest expeditions. In training for the invitation that never came he was known to walk from Liverpool to Wales for his climbing week-end.

By contrast, as has been seen, Menlove Edwards, once he attacked a cliff, did not rest until he had dissected it thoroughly. His explorations are spread over many years from the beginning of the 1930's well on into the forties and even fifties, with some of his finest achievements—the Bow-shaped Slab, Central Gully Direct on Lliwedd, Brant, Slape, and others—coming quite late in this period as he literally went from strength to strength. Inevitably in this enormous output of climbs there is a large proportion of dross; even his best routes have little design, but one climbs them for their excellent pitches, often somewhat improbably linked together. Perhaps he arrived at a time when the best fruit had fallen. 'Loose rock, vegetation, overhangs;

Menlove is a connoisseur.' Making due allowance for the difference in character, the standard of his climbs is closely similar to Kirkus's, steeper but shorter in the run-outs as a rule. Climbing has been by no means his sole form of expression, for he is a mountain writer who has rarely been equalled for evocativeness.

Kretschmer again:

Of great influence in the development of Welsh climbing was the appearance of the new series of climbing guide-books. The writing of guide-books in itself gave rise to much exploration, because the wide circulation of the detailed accounts of the new climbs spread the knowledge of these routes among many climbers. The new guide-books also produced a tendency towards specialization in rock climbing and caused to some extent its divorce from more general mountaineering whereby some lost the Welsh hills in a maze of rock climbs. [A very gratifying result if true, since it will help to keep the summits less crowded.] A new class of pure rock climbers sprang up, imbibing their knowledge of the hills almost entirely through the guide-books, and regarding the mountain setting of their sport as a more or less tiresome encumbrance.

Edwards's guide-book to Cwm Idwal was the first of this new series. This area had become the most frequented—because the most easily accessible—of all the Welsh climbing grounds. In this, some seventy-five routes were described on the Idwal Slabs and their walls, on the upper cliff of Glyder Fawr and Clogwyn y Geifr. Twenty-three of these were his own inventions. He followed this up in the next year with an equally full description of the climbs on Tryfan, a book in which Wilfrid Noyce, a new prodigy on the climbing scene, acted as co-editor; this work contributed, among other efforts, fine first leads of the Soap Gut, the Scars Climb, and the girdle of the Terrace Wall.

Colin Kirkus wrote the guide to Glyder Fach, and the contrast between this and the Edwards guide-books throws interesting light on the characters of their authors. In Kirkus's Glyder Fach guide, which is perhaps the best-liked and most useful guide-book for the average climber, we have the same system which Kelly used in the Lakeland guides, broadened and humanized perhaps, but essentially a type of description based on a system. This system was described by Edwards as the 'tiny narrow spotlight moving in a single line . . . the rocks might be any rocks and the conformation of the cliff and climb might be any conformation, might be any climb in mid air, for the spotlight sheds no rays aside. . . .' Kelly's main object in his Lakeland guide was to describe the climbs with the greatest possible clarity in the fewest possible words, assuming that the climber was not interested in literary style.   He wanted a system which would be consistent, easy of reference, and giving no scope to the fallible imagination of the compiler.   He accepted the fact that such a system must be based on purely artificial conventions and left the particular qualities of a route and its wider perspective to discover themselves to parties as they climbed.

In Edwards's guide we have nothing of this system, the basic principle being summed up in a single sentence in the introduction to his *Cwm Idwal*: 'It is hoped that the climber may get a good idea of things before ever seeing the cliff in question.'   This apparently simple and common-sense intention in fact meant a sharp break with the system because it introduced into guide writing the fact of the climber himself.   In 1939 Edwards's Lliwedd guide was published. This included more than eighty routes of which only thirty-six had been described in the original guide to Lliwedd, by J. M. Archer Thomson and A. W. Andrews, written in 1909.   During the war the Climbers' Club also published [provisional guide-books to] Clogwyn du'r Arddu, Craig yr Ysfa, and the three cliffs which lie on the Glyder side of the Llanberis valley (which continue to give their numerical name to all the climbing in the area, despite the fact that nearly a dozen cliffs are regularly climbed on in Llanberis).   The three cliffs are Dinas Cromlech, Clogwyn y Grochan, and Carreg Wastad.   Again Edwards was the chief, almost the only exploiter.

Suffice it to say here that subsequent Lakeland guides have followed in the Kelly, Welsh guides in the Edwards tradition, without nearly the difference in practice that all this furore might suggest.   The Welsh books are slightly more amusing to read in bed: but on the cliff there is nothing to choose, and the most important consideration for any guide is that it should fit in the hip pocket.   The Lakeland guides are enlivened by a list of all the climbs arranged in ascending order of difficulty, and while these are of course wildly inaccurate they provide all the fun of competition and give a great feeling of satisfaction to the aspiring climber ticking his way up the list.

To recap, then: during the early thirties the important explorations were on Cloggy, despite some good things done on the Ogwen side by Kirkus, Edwards, and, later, Noyce and Cox, and at Cwm Silyn by Kirkus. But while these Ogwen climbs often included pitches of difficulty fully equal to those of Cloggy or the Three Cliffs they lacked their length, continuity, and inescapability: they did not maintain the same average angle. Lliwedd was also being quietly finished off by various people, chiefly Longland at first and finally and most thoroughly by Edwards.

Longland has written: '[Lliwedd] remained a touchstone of Welsh climbing, the testing-piece set to visiting Lakeland experts or Gritstoneers, who, if they returned dejected or contemptuous after probing its peculiar virtues, were complacently written off as incomplete mountaineers.' That was in the late twenties: with the development of du'r Arddu, Lliwedd began to lose some of its attraction by comparison, and to a later generation of possibly incomplete mountaineers the idol seems, despite its impressive size and air of mystery, to have feet of clay, or at least to have been somewhat overestimated. The routes there do not define themselves much, and are all of a standard: the Severes and the Difficults seem uniformly easy in good weather and uniformly hard in bad. One can follow or abandon any climb either by chance or at will. It is undoubtedly a serious place and a great cliff, yet the actual climbs do not seem to match the cliff in quality. But in the thirties the trend was towards steeper climbs. Cloggy and the Three Cliffs began to come into their own. The genius of Edwards in the discovery and development of the latter must be emphasized: the future lay along these lines, and the first climbs here bear the relation of a prophecy to our time.

Kirkus's wonderful series on du'r Arddu was followed up by Linnell with his great Narrow Slab route in 1933, which shares the curiously formidable nature of so many of this leader's routes. In 1934–7 a brilliant Oxford group, initiated by John Hoyland and led by Robin Hodgkin and David Cox, repeated most of the routes and made some new ones of its own, accompanied on occasion by the daughters of George Mallory, Clare and Beridge. Hoyland's death in the Alps in 1934 robbed Welsh climbing of a climber of brilliance, who might have made notable contributions to its story. Edwards too made his route on du'r Arddu, but not until 1941: Bow-shaped Slab. Meanwhile, as we have seen, he had been working on Llanberis. Kretschmer says that:

The climbs on these cliffs require an expenditure of nervous energy considerably greater than that needed by the big routes on Clogwyn du'r Arddu. The ground sloping away at a steep angle below the crags, the fissile nature of the rock combined with the disappointment consequent on finding seemingly useful holds, rounded and inadequate when reached—all this contributes to producing a sense of apprehension in the cragsman.

Thus Kretschmer formulates a persistent myth. In fact, of course, a Very Severe pitch is Very Severe, whether it be in Ogwen, Llanberis, or Timbuctoo. The present writer is firmly of the opinion that any person out for a spree on nervous energy can find as good opportunities for extravagance on Cloggy as anywhere, and has never found the holds more disappointing on the Three Cliffs than elsewhere, while the possibilities for protection are generally greater. It is the old story of the ton of lead and the ton of feathers. Probably the impression was caused by the unaccustomed steepness of the cliffs—to-day Slape or Phantom Rib or Ribstone Crack seem no harder than Lot's Groove or Scars. 'It was a different sort of climbing, far in advance of the period in technique, much more vertical than the other in Wales.' Thus Harding. In fact, the vertical, so beloved of mountain writers, had up till then referred to a real angle of no more than sixty or seventy degrees. These Three Cliffs climbs began to press the right angle more closely, and the climber might expect to be confronted with walls of eighty or a bit more for as much as fifteen feet, and even genuinely overhanging rock without large holds for three or four. This was a big advance.

Across the valley, too, the future was germinating. 'The clean, steep rock of Dinas Mot was found to offer great satisfaction to some rock climbers and a sense of total inadequacy to others.' After an initial route or so by others, Kirkus stepped in and in 1930 made his magnificent Direct Route. The following year Edwards climbed his Western Slabs and Kirkus added another fine route of great fierceness, the West Rib, which was not to be excelled for delicacy for twenty years, and only equalled by

Arthur Birtwhistle's extraordinary Diagonal Route on the same cliff, put out in 1938. This last was perhaps the most remarkable for technique in Britain until the ascent of Suicide Wall on Glyder Fawr. Though perhaps containing no single move of greater difficulty than the hardest on West Rib, it multiplies them by six into a climb of sustained difficulty that belongs by nature more to the 1950's than to the thirties or even perhaps the forties. It is not at all artificial, but follows a line of weakness (if the word can be used) so delicately traced that in several places the removal of one tiny hold might make the climb impossible. Higher up Cwm Glas, people began to look at Craig Rhaiadr and Cyrn Las, and in 1935 Roberts and Cooke climbed the Main Wall of the latter, long thought to be impossible, and a masterpiece of route-finding, though in the event it turned out to be quite reasonable. This great route was promptly forgotten for ten years before being rediscovered.

Kretschmer continues:

Starting with E. Pentir Williams (the author of the elegant Sabre Cut of Dinas Cromlech) in the late twenties, local climbers became an important influence. The number of climbers, in a place like Bangor, is small, but reckoned per thousand it represents a much greater fraction of the population than does the number of climbers in London or Liverpool. Hal Jacob joined Williams in 1931 and these two climbed together nearly every week-end. They played only a small part in the exploration which took place in the thirties because they did not bother much about placing their activities on record and because they primarily climbed for the best reason of all—that is, for their own amusement. Another local climber was Jake Cooke [see above], who with P. L. Roberts climbed all the routes on Clogwyn du'r Arddu. Some of the local men like I. ap G. Hughes and that fine steady climber Scotty Dwyer, who has . . . become a professional guide, were closely associated with the youth hostel at Idwal. [This group, with whom must be included Dick Morsley, were responsible for the great Central Route on Llech Ddu in the Carneddau, one of Wales's best and most neglected climbs.] But there were many other brilliant performers, many of whom only made a brief début and then disappeared.

It is interesting to speculate on the advance in climbing technique and in climbing standards and to discover its cause. Advance there certainly was in the quality of difficulty, as well as in the evident

increase in the number of difficult climbs and the number of people
qualified to tackle them.   Judged by the sort of rock which still cannot
be climbed at all, the advance is slight.   We may think we do, but in
fact we do not climb up steep, clean, open faces.   If the rocks are really
open and the holds small, then the angle of the climb is not likely to
exceed sixty-five degrees, or if it does exceed it, as on the centre pitch
of the Great Slab on Clogwyn du'r Arddu, it will only do so for a few
feet at a time.   If the climb goes up rock which is really vertical or
overhanging, then it will have, fairly frequently, large spikes of rock
sticking out or it will remain unclimbed.   The advance in climbing
skill appears greater than it is, largely because the difficulty to be overcome in rock climbing is mainly subjective.   The difference in subjective difficulty between making a precarious movement at a point two
feet above safety as compared with a point sixty feet above safety is
tremendous.   It is this dealing with difficulty at a greater remove from
safety which distinguishes the hardest of the new climbs from the
hardest of the classic routes.   A good illustration of this is given by
Linnell's Narrow Slab route on Clogwyn du'r Arddu in comparison
with the Great Slab climb.   The former in some ways is perhaps the
most difficult all-round mountaineering feat of any of the North Welsh
climbs.   [This is rather a wild statement to have made, even at that
time.]   Yet there are a great many individual steps on other climbs
which are a great deal more difficult than anything found here, where
the route is nowhere unduly strenuous or extreme.   The unusual
feature of the climb is that it maintains a high level of difficulty
throughout.   In the steep middle section the difficulty actually
increases as the climb progresses, reaching its climax near the landing
at the top.   Each repetition of a climb will add to what is known about
it and in that way will reduce the difficulties presented to future parties.
This effect is particularly marked in the first half-dozen ascents of a
new route and in considering the advance in rock climbing this
phenomenon must be borne in mind.   In most cases objective difficulties presented by a climb will also tend to be reduced with each
ascent by the progressive removal of surplus vegetation and loose
rocks.   In some cases, however, the effect of wear and tear is to
increase difficulties through the removal of vital knobs and the
polishing of holds . . . rock climbing requires little specialized technique; it is a natural pursuit that will come easily to many healthy
persons.   Once the novice has learnt to stand on his feet, to use his
feet and go on using his feet and the strength of his legs, instead of
relying unduly on the strength of his arms, there is nothing much to

learn about performance. In matters of judgment, in distinguishing between safety and peril, this does not apply. Practice, however, is of great importance for strengthening muscles, increasing endurance, training the eye, and creating a large, quickly reacting situation memory. The eye accustomed to steepness will, without fuss, allow the adjustment necessary for equilibrium. It is the practised memory which will cause the use of the holds in the right combination, and only well-tuned muscles can give the confidence that stamps the expert rock climber. Some specialized technique must, however, be learnt; backing and kneeing, with one or two other tricks for chimney work and for levering the human body up cracks; then there is the general business of using holds by pressing—pressing upwards or from the side, rather than the obvious straight downward pull. The rest of climbing consists of using the muscles which are used ordinarily in the same sort of way.

For the moment we shall let this stand without comment. Let Kretschmer say his say:

The increase in the number of climbers also brought about an increase in the number of climbing mishaps. Although the dangers involved in rock climbing are nothing like as great as is suggested by the reporting of accidents in the more sensationalist sections of the popular press, the existence of certain objective and subjective risks must be admitted and they should be understood by all who climb. The First Aid Committee of Mountaineering Clubs, now renamed the Mountain Rescue Committee of Great Britain, have done much in educating the climbing public in how to deal with accidents. They have organized and equipped a series of first-aid points throughout the North Welsh climbing ground and they have worked out details of evacuation routes and rescue parties for all Welsh climbing areas. Details of these arrangements are included as an appendix in the series of climbing guides to the Snowdon district. All the [main] Welsh climbing clubs are now represented on this committee, which grew out of a sub-committee of the Rucksack Club set up in 1932 for devising better appliances and arrangements for dealing with accidents. To Fred Pigott, above all, belongs the credit for the fine organization which has evolved [and equally honourable mention must be made of the late Wilson Hey, climber and surgeon, who for many years equipped the first-aid rucksacks with morphia on his sole responsibility contrary to an unimaginative and inelastic law].

During the war the army invaded North Wales. The noise of firing and bombing reverberated in almost every valley.   Mountaineers who inadvertently got mixed up in battles were sometimes greeted by the soldiery with bullets and sometimes with the incredulous question: 'Are you really doing this for fun?'   There were several army climbing courses and there must have been occasions when instructors at these schools reached a higher standard of climbing fitness than anyone had before.   In 1945, C. Preston with a party spectacularly solved the old problem of the Suicide Wall in Cwm Idwal which had defeated both Edwards and Kirkus.

Short as it is, about one hundred feet, at that date it was the hardest climb in Wales, and even at the time of writing it has only been re-led twice.   Another climb, Advocate's Wall, was put out on the Devil's Kitchen cliffs by this army group, and yet a third was discovered on Clogwyn du'r Arddu by Jock Campbell and David Cox.   This route, the Sheaf, was a particularly daring first lead and ranks as one of the great routes of Wales.   It began as an attempt on the then unclimbed White Slab, but developed a line and a character of its own as it grew.   Preston heard that someone had run up Snowdon from Llanberis in under the hour, 'so after a day's climbing he ate a large steak pudding and ran up in forty-eight minutes and down in twenty-six and a quarter.' Haines of the same group reduced the record time for the circuit of the fourteen Welsh three-thousanders by an hour.   The story runs that:

It was hot for the time of year, so we wore only shorts and boots; half way round Jack Haines discarded the shorts and went on just in boots.   Someone clothed him to go through Nant Peris, but at Blaen y Nant he stripped again and sent a runner ahead to the top of Snowdon with his trousers.   He arrived, however, before the runner.   There were several ladies, including his wife, waiting at the top, and I heard later how his wife welcomed him with open arms while the others discovered a new beauty in the view of the Lleyn Peninsula.

Kretschmer concluded his chapter as follows:

Many now climb on the North Welsh cliffs; some are very good climbers and a talented newcomer often absorbs, in the space of one summer, the skill which took the most brilliant of his predecessors half a lifetime to acquire.   The majority, however, probably climb with a competence similar to that attained by the majority of climbers before the 1914 war, up routes of a similar standard of difficulty.

There have been changing fashions in ancillary equipment. The hard, sharp Tricouni nail succeeded the blunt clinker nail, then the fashion was reversed. From time to time the urge for self-expression produces fantastic patterns of nails. As in the Lakes, the rubber shoe has come into its own, in spite of the boot expert who protests that 'everything will go in nails.' The expert and the hardy sometimes use the stockinged foot on difficult passages and the exceptionally hardy climb barefooted, but that is a highly specialized technique. The use of pitons and other artificial climbing aids is rare in Wales and likely to remain so. Devices consisting of karabiners or snaplinks in combination with rope loops are often used for safeguarding the leader in exposed situations. Perhaps there is also a tendency to discard that quaint, traditional headgear of the British climber, the Balaclava helmet. . . . So in the space of less than ten years, North Wales . . . again [came] to the fore as the paramount rock-climbing ground in southern Britain. This development would probably have come in any case even without Kirkus and without Edwards, and yet their contribution stands out above all others. Not only did they between them make many more first ascents and discoveries than did all the other climbers together, during the whole period, but they did much to popularize rock climbing by teaching people, so that their direct influence has been, and is, felt by all outstanding rock climbers of recent times.

So far Kretschmer in 1947. One or two postscripts must be added before we move on to consider the post-war situation. First, mention must be made of John Barford and of Nully Kretschmer himself. Barford began climbing at Cambridge, but came to the fore only gradually, emerging into the limelight only just before the war. He was not a great maker of first ascents, but repeated most of the existing routes and wrote the interim guide-book to the Three Cliffs in Llanberis; he was also co-editor with Edwards of the interim du'r Arddu guide. But it is most of all as an organizing genius, as the man who held British mountaineering together during the war in his spare time from engineering, and who edited the Pelican book *Climbing in Britain*, that he will be remembered. He knew everybody and had a rare gift of getting things done: at the time of his death he was a key member of at least three major climbing organizations. Though he climbed everywhere North Wales was the scene of his greatest activity. Nully Kretschmer was also one of the most active and prominent climbers in the years just before and after the war. After co-editing the provisional Craig yr Ysfa guide with David Cox, and making his contribution of first ascents, he became General Guide-book Editor of the Climbers' Club and supervised the issue of all the volumes to the Cambrian cliffs. He was widely liked for his charm and character. Both Kretschmer and Barford were killed in tragic accidents in the Alps in the disastrously fine summer of 1947.

And last, it should be emphasized that the generation we have so far been discussing did all its climbing with hemp ropes, which if thick were prohibitively heavy, if thin were a negligible security, and were always awkward when wet or frozen. They used next to no pitons and very few running belays: karabiners only began to come in slowly after the mid thirties, and of course nylon line slings were undreamed of. Boots in those days necessarily meant nails, for vibrams had not made their appearance in conservative England. Young modern 'tigers,' repeating their climbs with all the modern rigmarole of safety, are sometimes heard to dismiss them as comparatively easy: yet how many of them would have done the first ascent of Diagonal Route, Lliwedd Central Gully Direct, Pedestal Crack, or the Narrow Slab on thin hemp line with few or no slings? The fact is that these climbs were masterpieces, unprecedented in their length of run-out, their exposure, continuity, and lack of protection, and in this last respect they are never likely to be excelled: they were as far ahead of the general level of the thirties as Llithrig or Cenotaph Corner are of the fifties, or nearly so. The greater number of persons now climbing hard routes is largely due to the improvement in methods of protection. Few have the force of heart and steadiness of will and muscle that these men displayed. The achievements of the generation may be summed up so: they undertook climbs of a much greater steepness and exposure than had hitherto existed, climbs of greater continuity of difficulty and grimness of aspect, and above all climbs on which the hardest moves came not ten but a hundred feet above the second man. The men of pre-1914 invented the balance technique of climbing, and the men of pre-1939 brought it to perfection. After the gully

8. Dinas Cromlech

epoch which ended about the turn of the century came the slab epoch. This may be said to have ended with the twenties, and was succeeded by a wall epoch. It was to be left to the climbers of the late forties, with their new equipment, to perfect this in their turn. In 1950 the technique of out-of-balance climbing came into its own, and the overhang epoch began. One might also make out a case for a crack epoch. Such cut-and-dried definitions are naturally over-simplified, yet they may have some value if accepted with due reservation. These later events we shall now review.

3

It is a truism that war, though causing boundless tragedy and decidedly not worth it, accelerates material progress. From the point of view of the British rock climber there can be no doubt that the most important thing to come out of the war was the invention of nylon rope and an abundance of cheap karabiners. To the Alpine climber the mass introduction of vibram boot soles and the discovery of the virtues of down-filled clothing were perhaps of equal significance, but these innovations had no direct influence on the course of mountaineering in Wales, whereas the all-out use of the nylon sling and karabiner was to be revolutionary. Nylon is far lighter for a given strength than hemp, owing to its resilience, and it has the added advantage that, being impermeable, it remains light and supple in all weather conditions. However, it has the unfortunate characteristic that it melts at a very low temperature, and hence that it frays easily. It is vital that no moving rope should ever be allowed to run across stationary nylon: but before this lesson was properly learned there were unfortunate accidents, notably on the Munich climb on Tryfan. But because it is so strong and light, it is possible to manufacture it usefully in some very thin diameters, and a piece about three times the thickness of a normal shoe-lace will support the weight of a thousand pounds. Owing partly to the spiky character of Welsh rock it has become the fashion for leaders to carry increasingly large numbers of loops of this thin

G

nylon line, each fitted with a karabiner.   These are left hooked over spikes of rock or threaded behind stones jammed in cracks, with the leader's rope running through the karabiner, and are known as running belays, or just runners.   As soon as a leader has clipped his rope into one of these his situation is materially changed, for if he then peels off he will only have to fall twice the distance to his runner, instead of twice the distance to his second man, before coming on the rope.   The difference between these two prospects when faced by a hard move or a stretch of loose rock a hundred feet above one's second has to be experienced to be believed.   Nowadays where runners are lacking pitons are often used for the same purpose, and while there is an undoubted loss to heroism there is a compensatory gain to common sense and pleasure.

When Nully Kretschmer began his survey of pre-war and war-time climbing he did so by mentioning certain men first, as the first cause of progress.   It will be noted that I have begun with material.

Once hostilities had ceased, it did not take long for a new generation to appear.   Bred mostly on gritstone, its Welsh habitat was the Llanberis Pass.   The first to emerge was John Lawton, a genial and highly muscular climber already in his mid thirties, whose climbing career had been interrupted by the war. Though he contributed comparatively few new routes of his own, Lawton was responsible for the second ascent of many of the top-class routes that had been put up between 1938 and 1946, and was a major influence in the reopening up of the area for exploration. His great determination was illustrated by his first ascent of the Suicide Groove on the East Wall of the Idwal Slabs, which at the time of writing has been repeated only once.   Most unfortu-nately he suffered a serious accident on Clogwyn y Grochan in 1949 from which he was extremely lucky to escape alive, and which left him a weakened arm and a completely inflexible ankle that put paid to more extreme explorations, but happily he is still an active climber.   On one occasion, to the knowledge of the present writer, though he had arrived by motor-cycle from England only the night before, he left Chamonix on a baking hot morning, and having ascended to Planpraz walked all the way to

Lac Blanc, then up to the foot of the appropriately named Aiguille de la Persévérance (at this point one fit member of the party dropped out), whence he climbed the difficult north-north-east *arête* and then descended all the way to Chamonix the same evening. Unimpeded members of the party were worn out coming down through the dark steep woods, but John stumped cheerfully into Chamonix on his lame foot at 11 p.m. obviously unperturbed.

But the great men of this generation in Wales were undoubtedly Peter Harding and Tony Moulam, supported by Dave Thomas, Peter Hodgkinson, and John Disley the Olympic steeplechaser. Harding and Moulam both followed the usual course of Welsh tigers by starting their climbing careers on gritstone. Both were members of the Derbyshire Stonnis Club, and between them they were responsible for a very large number of first ascents on the southern edges. Harding was the quicker to develop, and from 1947 to 1949 he literally plastered the walls of the Llanberis Pass with new climbs, carrying on the work that Edwards had begun. The superficial resemblance between his climbing and Edwards's is remarkable, and perhaps springs from a certain similarity of physique, for Harding is also a man of medium height, powerful build, and long arms. His manner of climbing was slow and deliberate as a rule. Again, his tendency (though more limited than Edwards's in time and extent) was to concentrate on a limited area and to work it out exhaustively, though for this we must probably partly blame the extreme thoroughness with which earlier generations had worked out the Ogwen valley and their equally striking neglect of Llanberis. Though he was an all-round technician the character of the area he chose, combined, perhaps, with a physical predisposition, led him towards the Great Overhang and the Vice-like Hand Jam. His great contribution to the climbing history of Wales was to combine the standards of the greatest pre-war climbers with the new materials and techniques in order to exploit climbs perhaps more difficult and sustained and steep relative to their apparent exposure than most that Wales had seen up to that time, and it may be said that he made an advance in the standard of crack climbing. It was important for the future of Welsh rock climbing that he had a mind singularly free from the old prejudice against artificial aids and protection.   In 1948 he wrote:

> This article would be incomplete without an attempt to rekindle the old flame of controversy.   Pitons!   Pegs!   Bergstaples!   Call them what you will—a rose by any other name—and there would still be the same old question, to be or not to be.   At one time in this country rubbers were looked upon in much the same way as pegs are regarded by some climbers to-day.   Climbing in rubbers is now an accepted and even desirable practice; which shows the triumph of common sense over prejudice.   I feel sure that . . . the British rock climber will soon catch up with the Continentals in the very specialized and skilled section of mountain craft known as piton work.   In the past, whenever pitons have been mentioned, a mental picture has sprung up of fanatical Nazis rawlplugging their way up the Eigerwand [a quaint conception].   We have said 'That isn't mountaineering!' but it is a technique in the solution of mountaineering problems, just as much as is the use of chock-stones, lassoing, or shoulders.

Though things have moved slowly and with moderation, the trend here predicted by Harding has undoubtedly been taking place and will probably continue.

His period of major exploratory activity may be said to have begun in May 1947 with the powerful first ascent of the Spectre on Clogwyn y Grochan, which will always remain one of the finest routes in the valley though long since deposed from its position as the most difficult climb.   In August of the same year he led the Ivy Sepulchre on Dinas Cromlech, a route of great singleness and verticality which had defeated all previous attempts.   The following summer saw numerous routes going up along the walls of the valley, his outstanding feat of the year being perhaps Kaisergebirge Wall, a short but very exposed and difficult climb: perhaps the most difficult of all his climbs.   But it must be noted that although these routes exceeded the majority of previous ones in the sort of fierceness caused by difficulty relative to apparent exposure they all necessitated the use of pitons as well as slings, and that pre-war climbers considered the use of such aids as in general unfair and debarred.   Coming in a still later generation the present writer applauds their use in these cases, and the force of character required to disregard the prejudice against them.   But it is also clear that, though the average level is higher, none of these climbs contains any intrinsic difficulties which might not have been surmounted by the best of the pre-war climbers had all these aids existed or had they allowed themselves the use of them —physically they could have passed—and this for a reason which I have not seen explicitly set out elsewhere. It relates to the phrase which I have used above, apparent exposure. When the novice climber comes into a very open position he feels as exposure all the distance that is between him and the ground. The expert climber, however, knows that the real amount of exposure is that between him and the nearest reliable running belay or piton, and can disregard the further irrelevant number of hundred feet below as merely apparent exposure in all but the most extreme cases, or even in them. Kaisergebirge Wall is a perfect example of what I mean. The crux of this climb is poised above a rigorously vertical wall of perhaps sixty feet, at the bottom of which is the ground, strewn with boulders. The climber has a tiny ledge on which to collect his forces. Then he has to make several moves up a vertical groove on holds which are small and awkwardly spaced. He has to work the moves out first and then make up his mind and climb quickly, for few people have the strength to rest on or retreat down such small holds at such an angle. In other words he has to commit himself: it is this necessity which distinguishes the XS from the VS grading. The number of people who could lead such a climb safely on sight without protection is very small indeed in 1956. But fortunately the climber has a choice of several running belays and piton cracks which reduce the exposure to a bearable level by more or less guaranteeing that if he has overestimated his abilities and falls off he will not suffer any serious harm. This fact has contributed to the popularity of the climb among the best leaders, and the confidence thus induced enables the aspiring climber to think coolly, try really determinedly, and so climb well. Even so the proportion of mountaineers who have led it is small, though there are many who have made moves of comparable difficulty close to the ground, as on, for example, the first pitch of Diphthong on Gimmer Crag in the Lake District, or Hermitage Crack at Cratcliffe Tor, which is graded Very Difficult: yet with intelligence and even one piton Kaisergebirge Wall can be rendered almost as safe, and the great difference is the apparent exposure. In difficulty related to real exposure, exposure to damage, Kirkus's West Rib of Dinas Mot ranks higher.

In 1949 Harding brought his great campaign to a close with more routes on the Three Cliffs, notably the Lion, Unicorn, his beautiful Direct Start to Edwards's Brant, and the Green Cater-pillar on Cyrn Las. The climax of his deeds was the girdle traverse of the West Buttress of Clogwyn du'r Arddu, which was an expedition of a length and continued difficulty unmatched in Wales, giving seven or more Very Severe pitches and over a thousand feet of climbing, and which fittingly symbolized his high place in the hierarchy of home mountain explorers. Much praise on this feat must also go to his second, Gordon Dyke, a fellow member of both the Climbers' and the Stonnis clubs, who did most of the climb with a sprained wrist. The girdle wanders up the Sheaf, down across the easy upper part of Narrow and round on to the Bow; then it reverses the traverse of the Bow and goes across to and up the Forty Foot Corner of the Great Slab, up Central Rib and then out across three hundred feet of traverse (which was then new ground) 'to finish in a grassy chimney way out on the western sky-line': a masterpiece of climbing and route-finding, and a fitting end to an era. It represented the completion and familiarization of the great du'r Arddu classics, and was the last word in what could be done without a new standard of climbing.

The climbing career of A. J. J. Moulam has been less concen-trated both in time and in space. He began coming to Wales from his native Derbyshire at the same time as Harding, and in the succeeding years worked quietly and methodically through all the existing routes, sometimes seconding Harding in his explorations, but not contributing much of importance until 1950, and thus overlapping with a later period. He is of medium height and build, and has a technician's approach, perhaps owing to his two bad knees, neither of which can be bent very far: like Harding he climbs slowly and carefully, and has the distinction, probably unique in an explorer of his standing, of never having fallen off while leading a rope. While at Manchester University he spent all his spare time in the hills, and was thus able to complete the

9. Clogwyn du'r Arddu

Photo by J. K. Edwards

climbing guide-book to the Carnedds which so many had taken up only to leave off, and more recently he has rewritten the Tryfan and Glyder Fach guides into one volume. This ubiquity is typical of his climbing. In April 1951 he put up his short but excellent Ribstone Crack on Carreg Wastad, and in May with Geoff Pigott added the Bole Way to the same cliff. The following year he was the first to put his own guide-book out of date by giving the Carneddau their finest route, Mur y Niwl, on the hitherto unclimbed Lower Amphitheatre Wall of Craig yr Ysfa. This climb was modern in its conception in that it necessitates the use of pitons, but if ever climb were a justification for their use this is it: the climb is, and will surely always remain, one of the finest for position in Britain. Its discovery and first ascent on a misty day were triumphs of route-finding ability and determination. The standard is roughly that of Brant or Slape, but in a position more sensational than any of the pre-Brown routes on Clogwyn du'r Arddu, and the combination of this climb with the Pinnacle Wall above will always provide one of the best mountain days that Britain has to offer. Later in 1952 Moulam solved another old problem, the Ogof Direct at Cwm Silyn. Apart from these two outstanding routes Moulam was one of the leading explorers of the comparatively little-known cliffs above Tan y Grisiau, and at Tremadoc, on Craig y Bere, Craig Cwm Dulyn, the Rivals, all over the Carnedds, and on many another unheard-of crag. Many of these are very good routes that deserve to become more widely known, and have lifted the cliffs they adorn straight from the embryonic state into maturity. This was especially so at Tremadoc, where there was not a single rock climb before Easter 1951: yet to-day the cliffs are networked with climbs of a high standard.

Other prominent members of what one cannot help thinking of as the Harding generation were, as I have mentioned before, Hodgkinson, Thomas, and Disley, all of whom have various new climbs to their credit. It was a feature of the climbing of these men that they frequently did in nails what had hitherto been regarded as rubber climbs, which is an indication of great technique, or great fitness in the fingers, or both. Hodgkinson and Disley are slim and wiry, but Thomas is enormous, and the sight of him tiptoeing up a slab or assaulting an overhang is a very majestic spectacle indeed—nevertheless, as his record proves, a highly efficient one.   At this time, too, there were some very powerful climbers at the older universities.   Michael Ward and the late Tom Bourdillon, from Cambridge and Oxford respectively, made a crop of new climbs and variations which would have been larger if they had not departed shortly afterwards to more picturesque surroundings in search of bigger game.   Ward is a climber of studied elegance and beautiful technique.   Probably no one will ever know just how much virgin rock was covered by Bourdillon, owing to his habit of wandering happily and eccentrically all over a cliff in search of some perfectly obvious pitch, wanderings in which, to judge from the report of his seconds, his titanic strength must have been a very comforting asset.   One of the most remarkable of all university rock climbers was Mervyn Hughes of Oxford. · He has never bothered to record much of what he did, but among the remarkable feats he performed were the second ascent of the Spectre when totally out of condition (his first climb for months) and the solo first ascent of the still harder Overlapping Wall.   He also made many forays into unfrequented cwms and crags, and his wiry, pale, and slightly sinister figure might have been seen flitting up rocks of great difficulty, most of which have never found their way into any guide-book, in remote corners of Cwm Silyn, Clogwyn y Geifr, the Teyrn Bluffs, and Craig Cwm Ffynnon Lloer.   From Cambridge came Cym Smith, who gave brief and brilliant promise for the future by making ascents of most of the existing routes, often in bad conditions, and then adding a couple of his own before his tragic death in a road accident.   There is little doubt that but for this his name would have bulked large in this chapter.   In general the eyes of the varsity men were turned more to the Alps, where they began to carry out some remarkable campaigns, and to the Himalaya.   But if the arrow's tip was formed by the Northerners, much of the weight in the head just behind it came from the O.U.M.C. and the C.U.M.C., and the difference was largely a matter of the availability of the rocks.

At this time (and, indeed, since the early forties) a great generation of climbers had been at work in the Lake District, producing routes harder than, if not so great in scale as any Wales had to offer. The most notable leaders of this generation were Birkett and (coming slightly later) Dolphin. Birkett confined his attentions almost exclusively to the Lakes, but Dolphin paid various visits to Wales and climbed all the important routes until 1951. In the course of one of these visits he made his only contributions to the Welsh repertory in the form of the block finish to the Milestone Buttress, and two short but very difficult routes on the Terrace Wall of Tryfan which brought this excellent little piece of rock to its final maturity. Thus we arrive at the climbing situation very much as it existed on New Year's Day 1951.

Since the war the enthusiasm for mountains, and (not always connected) for making a name on the rocks, has become more widespread than ever before. The number of people coming to the Welsh hills with the intention of using a rope has seemed to double itself every two or three years since 1946. Age cannot wither nor custom stale their infinite variety: they are of every shape and age and ideal and sex and condition of life—greeting them on the hill it is fascinating but vain to speculate whether the reply will come in the most dulcet of Oxford modulations or a good outright adenoidal scowse. In only one thing are they uniform, and that is their appearance. During the war numbers of wind-proof camouflaged smocks and trousers, karabiners and ice-axes were produced to serve our men in bloodthirsty battles on mountain tops and icebergs which fortunately never took place. Since that time they have been made inexhaustibly available, at an ever-increasing profit, to the fortunate climbing public: and indeed it is true to say that, if drab, they are practical, strong, and were once cheap. Of recent years a strain of dandyism has become visible, probably as a result of visits to elegant Chamonix, but if a climber got himself somehow mixed up in a caravanserai he might still expect to be accosted with:

> 'But who are ye in rags and rotten shoes,
> Ye filthy-bearded, blocking up the way?'

Indeed this more or less happened to one party who visited the Hoggar mountains a few years ago. But happily for most of us who take any notice of our appearance at all, the great brown beards bending over into immeasurable space, the lines and curls of the wind-blown hair, the delicate undulations of the fissured anorak, are old and trusted friends.   They are likely to remain so as long as Welsh weather and Welsh cliffs and Welsh turf remain what they are, for there is small point in going out in creased trousers or linen shirt to bury one's arms up to the elbows in muddy cracks or to back and foot up through a waterfall—and for those who camp or stay in club huts shaving takes up too much valuable sleeping time.   At any rate it is probably true to say that while the average climber to-day may have almost anything on his head or his feet, between them he will be wearing old cord or flannel bags, a sweater or two and a camouflaged anorak.

Many of these hordes of climbers stay at the youth hostels at Idwal and elsewhere, or at the cottages of the Holiday Fellowship, and still more camp.   An increasingly large number are being attracted by the training courses offered by bodies such as the Central Council for Physical Recreation.   These organizations for a fee take complete charge of the mountaineer or would-be mountaineer, house him (or her), feed him, and train him competently according to his level in all the lore, and often a good deal besides, that mountains might possibly require of him.   Most of the best and keenest beginners eventually find their way into one or other of the clubs, of which there is now a variety exactly corresponding to the variety of climbers.   Many of these are new and still small, and a large proportion have particular affiliations. Thus every university now has its own club, so do all the services and practically every town of any size, at least north of Birmingham.   Some are open to all, some have local or technical qualifications, many of them are highly active: but though most have their tigers few of them have a high overall climbing standard. Such a statement is of course relative, and the number of people now leading climbs in their first year which were once considered difficult is astonishing.   A distinguished rock climber seems to have summarized the matter rather well in the following words:

My own novitiate lasted years and is I think still with me.   I surely had as little inborn aptitude for shinning up steep rock as an elephant; but I bore in mind the old saying that it took six years to make a

10. Joe Brown on the East Buttress, Clogwyn du'r Arddu

climber, and tried not to be discouraged by my clumsiness. It seemed better to learn slowly, but surely and safely.

That however does not appear to happen nowadays. I don't know any novices; nobody seems to be a novice, ever. The usual thing is for a beginner to go on the rocks at Easter and lead Lot's Groove at Whit Week; and one could never call such people novices. As for fear—why, the veriest lads at Laddow gambol up and across Tower Face, as carefree as Ogwen goats. At the ages of eighteen and twenty these young men are considered senior and experienced, and are highly thought of by fifteen-year-olds who have done nothing harder than North Wall, at least not as a lead. I, at twenty-eight, now feel senile and out of place on what I used to regard as much my crag as anybody's. If I hesitate for a second on the scoop on Long Climb, some peach-down-lipped tiger half way up Leaf Buttress finds time to look down and point kindly to the high sloping foothold on the left. 'It's quite easy,' he says.

I was sitting in the Pulpit at Laddow a few weeks ago with two youngsters. In my younger days they would have been called novices. On the top end of their rope was a member of the club whom I have venerated for years as a master of rockcraft and a performer of great deeds. A pioneer, in fact. I mentioned his name to them, lowering my voice suitably, and hoping they would be fittingly impressed. 'Who's he?' they said. 'Never heard of him!' Yet one of these two, so ignorant of the History of Climbing and so unimpressed by the presence of the Great, later led me up the most desperate piece of rock on which I have ever torn my fingernails. Earlier in the day, I had seen this boy in front of me in a bus queue, and had wondered where his mother was and why she allowed him to go out alone.

Outstanding among the new clubs has been the Rock and Ice Club, to which we shall have cause to revert presently; and Bristol University has begun to add itself to the number of university clubs (hitherto largely Manchester, Oxford, and Cambridge) which have made significant contributions to Welsh climbing. Because of the excellent limestone and granite climbing available in the south-west (a fact which has only just begun to be realized and exploited) it is possible that the northerners may not in future enjoy such a monopoly of exploration in Wales as they have done for the last thirty years. The older and larger clubs have gone from strength to strength. The numbers

of the Climbers' Club have increased to over six hundred, yet the
club has succeeded in remaining friendly and is one of the most
active in Britain both for home and foreign climbing.   It now
owns three huts in Wales and one in Cornwall and is responsible
for guide-book production to these areas.   Its journal is the
acknowledged repository of information about new climbs in
Snowdonia and Cornwall.   Equally thriving and active are the
Rucksack and Wayfarers' Clubs, the former of which owns a hut
in Llanberis Pass: and the Pinnacle Club, the Midland Association
of Mountaineers, and the Cromlech Club all provide one hut each
for the convenience of their members, while a host of smaller
groups lay more or less claim to shelters of a more rough-and-
ready kind.   For some years the Caernarvonshire County
Council thoughtfully provided a road-menders' hut near Pont y
Cromlech, but to the tribulation of hundreds this has now been
moved to a site nearer Caernarvon, and only a mound of empty
baked-bean tins remains to record its passing.   There are also
some excellent shelter stones in the district—but far be it from me
to spread the knowledge of their whereabouts.

Before the turn of the century most climbers drank their ale at
Pen y Gwryd.   Then the fashion changed, and they drank it
instead at Pen y Pass until about 1930.   Between then and the
end of the war one presumes they still drank it somewhere, but
they don't seem to have been terribly downright about it.   Since
1947, however, there has been no ambiguity at all: with the
exception of the Liverpool group at Idwal, whom bus schedules
have confined to Capel Curig, they have drunk it at Pen y Gwryd.
The wheel has turned full circle.   This state of affairs is evidently
going to continue as long as the present landlord, Chris Briggs,
who has done so much for the perpetual cheer and periodic rescue
of the climber in Wales.   No study of post-war climbing would
be complete without due emphasis on Pen y Gwryd as its social
background.   Since it was the birth-place of Welsh climbing
nothing could be more appropriate, and within its hospitable walls
tradition and talk of the latest explorations mingle agreeably.

I have already mentioned the post-war guide-books to Ogwen
and the Carnedds.   There was nothing in those areas to necessi-
tate any break with tradition, and the books follow agreeably and

competently in what may be called the 'diluted Edwards' system. The manifesto of the generation of the late forties, however, was the guide to Llanberis Pass.   In this volume (which contained a quantity of difficult climbs hitherto unparalleled) Harding drew attention to the fact that the variations in difficulty embraced by the grade Very Severe were now as great as those comprised by all the other grades together.   His remedy for this was to introduce two new gradings: Extremely Severe and Exceptionally Severe.   In retrospect it seems that one of these would have been sufficient, for the hardest XS's in the Llanberis guide are hardly more than hard Very Severe by the standards of 1956, and climbs fully two grades harder have been made of recent years without an increase in the number of superlatives in the English language; so that we are faced with the anomaly of the Sickle (say), which, although as hard as the Spectre, has been graded two standards lower by its modest author.   An attempt to solve this sort of muddling was made by Barford in his earlier guide to the Three Cliffs in Llanberis, and in other interim guides published at the same time.   This consisted of the substitution of numbers for adjectives in the grading of climbs.   English sentiment and lack of logic was responsible for the rejection of this method of grading; but in fact it had not marked any advance on the adjectival system, for (quite apart from the form adopted being absurdly complicated) it swallowed whole the essential fallacy of the old order.   The weak point is revealed in both systems at the top, where in each case it was found necessary to set aside one standard (Exceptionally Severe or Grade VI) for climbs which, in addition to being difficult, were long, sustained, exposed, or loose.   Thus we find one form of symbol simultaneously representing two entirely distinct kinds of data.   Inevitably their conflicting demands caused anomalies: Balcony Cracks, with perhaps three feet of Very Severe rock (but what do we mean by Very Severe?), virtual lack of exposure, and pitches artificially avoiding easy ground is graded the same as Great Slab, with its several hundred feet of serious and inescapable climbing, much of it on suspect material: the hardest movements of both routes are much of a standard, yet one is manifestly a harder thing to climb than the other.   Or the contradiction in terms reveals itself the other way about, and a climb is overgraded in difficulty because of exposure: or we find an author squirming, a verbal Houdini, with remarks like 'Just Very Severe owing to the serious nature of the climb and its intimidating overhang. The technical difficulty is much lower but that does not justify a lower classification. Under bad conditions the climb can be quite difficult.' Substitution of numbers and adjectives cannot provide a cure for this kind of malady. The answer is, of course, that if we have two sets of data we must have two sets of symbols to represent them. The data may be summed up under the headings of the difficulty, pure and simple, of each pitch in normal conditions: and the overall character of the climb, taking account of length, exposure, continuity of difficulties, the quality and usual condition of the rock, possibilities for protection and so on. The method adopted in the Vallot Guide to the range of Mont Blanc does not seem to have been bettered anywhere, and it is hard to see how it could be improved upon. It consists, brilliant in its simplicity, in grading each pitch numerically and the whole climb adjectivally, with a short description to explain its reasons. This method would be easily applicable to Wales. Further, the grading of a climb in the Vallot Guide is not based on the opinion of an individual, but that of a symposium of experts. But to return: in other respects the Llanberis guide also follows in the diluted Edwards tradition, and has been a popular and trusted stand-by to the generation whose atmosphere and achievements it evokes.

4

Towards the end of the forties, rumours of strange happenings began to circulate through the more active part of the climbing world. A gritstone problem that had baffled the top-roped tigers of three generations had been led on sight by a mere lad, or the same lad, having 'appeared to experience very little difficulty,' would proceed to haul some harassed and hard-breathing climbing immortal behind him up a climb regarded as solely for the very elect. Then the rumours ceased for a time, and many people began to forget them, or considered their subject to have been just another flash in the pan. In reality he was in the Far East, doing his National Service. In 1951, on his demobilization, the lad came to Wales: a crop of new climbs began to appear in Llanberis and on Clogwyn du'r Arddu in places where it had never seriously occurred to anyone before that possible lines might exist, and it was generally obvious that a new star had risen in the climbing firmament. The name of this star was Joe Brown. Other climbers who had hitherto been considered at the very top of the ladder tried to repeat his climbs (often in good conditions where the first ascent had been done in bad) and failed, or perhaps with difficulty they managed one or two of the easiest ones. Quickly it became apparent that rock climbing had taken another major jump forward, and that even taking all modern aids into account the new climbs were not only more exposed and sustained than any that had been done before, but more difficult— much more difficult. For the first time physical specialization began to make itself evident. Up to this time there had been great climbers of every build: though there was a numerical bias in the direction of men of medium height and wiry or muscular frame, the hardest climbs had been available to and had been done by men of every build who possessed the necessary technique and determination. It is dangerous to make predictions, but it seems probable that future advances in rock climbing will be made by men of less than medium height but of strong and lithe physique, for apart from other considerations only such men have the power-to-weight ratio necessary, above all in the fingers, to climb safely up the angles and minute holds of new ultra-Severes. This theorizing is borne out in practice by the fact that only four or five men have (up to 1956) climbed at the top-class modern level, and they are all of the build I have described. It is curious that while they have nearly all made their mark in the Alps (unlike so many of the best climbers of the two previous decades) their explorations in Wales have been almost exclusively on Clogwyn du'r Arddu and the immediate environs of Llanberis.

Brown started the ball rolling in 1951 (he was then twenty years old) with his ascent of the Hangover on Clogwyn y Grochan, and quickly began to follow up with his extraordinary series of climbs on the East Buttress and the Pinnacle of du'r Arddu, a series never perhaps even equalled elsewhere in the history of the sport, certainly never bettered. The Diglyph climb came first, in June, and Vember and the Boulder followed in the autumn, both of which had been tried by various people, with conspicuous lack of success; and on the latter route nobody was able to follow the second pitch so that the leader was forced to finish it alone. The following year came the Black Cleft (on which the lead was shared with Whillans) in May; Llithrig, Octo, the Corner, the Pinnacle Flake, and the Spillikin in June. Probably such a month's activity has never been seen on a British crag, yet at the same time and previously other routes had been going up on the Llanberis cliffs as well, notably (in 1951) the Cemetery Gates, shared with Whillans, and in 1952 Jericho Wall, Canol, and finally Cenotaph Corner on Dinas Cromlech. This had become something of a symbol and a last great problem, and its ascent in damp conditions was an extreme *tour de force*. Its author thought it the hardest of his new climbs. In 1953 came some new climbs on Cyrn Las of major importance, the Subsidiary Groove, on which he again shared the lead with Whillans, and the Grooves. He seems to have been running out of names for all these new climbs about this time. Clogwyn y Grochan was filled in with two more very hard routes, the Sickle and the Surplomb, in which last Whillans once again shared the honours. The campaign on du'r Arddu was brought to a climax with the ascents of the East Gully Wall, the Gargoyle, the Carpet Slab on the West Buttress, and the greatest achievement of all, the girdle traverse of the East Buttress (Whillans sharing the two last named, with, on the girdle, J. R. Allen as middle man). This expedition comprises 780 feet of climbing, much of it in the extreme category. It was started at 6.30 a.m. and finished by lunch-time. Letters received at this time make it all sound almost dull: 'We saw —— on Cloggy the other Saturday and on the Sunday we managed to do the girdle of the East, it took us six and a half hours.' Or (Carpet Slab): 'We did a new route on Cloggy the week-end after the dinner. It goes up the break to the right of the Red Slab. It is 250 feet long, graded hard VS. We had to use a peg to climb the bulge about 20 feet above the start. After the first 70 feet it is almost all grass. Still very interesting.' But the magnitude of the achievements underlying this modesty needs no underlining. These routes largely made use of the great bare walls between the obvious breaks which had provided all the original routes. The wall of the Pinnacle overlooking the East Gully, which looks the acme of inaccessibility, was also yielding a surprising number of climbs, though its appearance is so discouraging that it had never even been considered before. This refusal to be deterred by appearances is one of the characteristics of Brown's and Whillans's climbing.

Whillans joined in the hunt at an early stage and contributed many routes of his own in addition to the ones enumerated above. Outstanding examples are the Red Wall of Craig Rhaiadr, the Erosion Grooves of Carreg Wastad (perhaps the finest natural line on the crag, and probably the hardest), and the East Gully Grooves on du'r Arddu. He and Brown climbing together have formed by far the most formidable team ever to operate on British crags, and indeed perhaps anywhere else, as they have demonstrated in the Alps.

In 1953 Moseley appeared on the pioneering scene, and, having repeated some of the Brown climbs, made the Boulder Left Edge and Moss Groove climbs on du'r Arddu, both of which are very fine lines. Moss Groove takes the corner on the right of the Great Slab, between it and the Central Rib. The crag was rapidly growing into its maturity. One or two more deeds on it must, however, be mentioned.

There was at this time a flowering of the Cambridge club, probably partly as a result of the influence of Cym Smith. The eyes of this Cambridge generation, led by the tall and lanky figure of George Band,[1] were turned principally towards the Alps, as is the Cambridge tradition. However it was very active in Wales also, and indeed at this time it was probably about the most active group after the Rock and Ice Club group of Brown and his associates Whillans, Moseley, Allen, Sorrel, and others. In the same June that Brown made Llithrig and all the other routes he had looked at the Red (or Bloody) Slab on the western end of the West Buttress and, like many another great climber before him,

[1] Who with Joe Brown was the first to climb Kangchenjunga.

H

had decided it would not go. This was probably only a remark and not his considered opinion, but at any rate it went, only a few days later. The successful climber was John Streetly of the C.U.M.C.

Early in his Cambridge career Streetly had unfortunately been put off climbing by some damping remarks made by a well-known climber who did not appreciate the extent of his potentialities. In the spring of 1952, however, shortly before he was due to go down, Ted Wrangham, another Cambridge climber possessed of a persuasive tongue, a forceful personality, and several fast cars, cajoled him into revisiting the cliffs. In two or three week-ends he made rapid ascents of a number of the hardest climbs on Stanage, Almscliff, and Harrison's Rocks, on which last he was observed by the writer hanging from an overhang with one hand while cleaning the soles of his rubbers with the other. He was taken to Wales and promptly led the Spectre (still retaining the aura of a difficult climb in those days), including a new variation, in a total climbing time of eighteen minutes. Shortly after, with Band, he made the second ascents of Mur y Niwl (with a new direct start to the Pinnacle Wall), the girdle traverse of the West Buttress of Clogwyn du'r Arddu, and a number of other routes of equal or greater difficulty in the space of a few days. In the interim blue guide to Clogwyn du'r Arddu J. M. Edwards made an understatement which has become famous: 'One would not advise a beginner to lead here too immediately.' Streetly, however, having done the girdle on his first visit, proceeded to lead the Red Slab on his second, one of the most difficult new routes on the cliff according to Brown, who made the second ascent. After which this meteor (in whose life climbing had played such a brief and minor part) paid a short but notable visit to the Alps and disappeared into the wilds of his native Trinidad. There have been many meteors in the climbing firmament who have blazed for a year or two and then passed over to other horizons leaving behind them a world of dazzled envious eyes— one thinks of Roper, Balcombe, and Preston among others—but surely never one to equal this in swiftness and brilliance and promise.

Streetly's description of this climb is, so far as I know, the only existing frank account of one of the really hard modern climbs, and it may be of interest to quote a little (see Plate 12(*a*)):

From here on the climb became quite thin and now it is difficult to recall how the next thirty feet were managed at all. At one stage the only means of moving up was by reaching at full stretch with the right hand to finger-jam in the bottom of a vertical crack about eighteen inches long and half an inch wide. By pulling up on this and then body-leaning to the left it was possible to swing up to the level of the top of the crack. At this critical point a quick call from an ever-watchful second pointed to the only possible foothold about two feet away to the left. This allowed a moment's respite in a more or less bridged position which, itself being very tiring and with the previous move being apparently impossible to reverse, left no alternative but to go on up. With the difficult move below and the uncertainty of what was still to come, life at this point seemed to depend more upon faith than friction.

Still, after the second runner, the slab was dry and tiny flakes allowed pleasantly delicate finger and toe climbing to lead to a some-what doubtful flake behind which the placement of the only piton manufactured another runner. This was about seventy feet from the start and about a hundred feet from the rake directly below with still no possibility of a stance, belay, or even a resting-place. About fifteen feet above was the first large overhang in the middle of the slab and the third runner made for much more confident climbing up to the base of this. At this point the first real handhold of the climb was manufactured by extensive gardening in the crack immediately below the overhang. Here the general dampness and moss made rubbers both useless and dangerous, so they had to be removed quickly and tucked away in case they were necessary later on. The climb was continued in socks, and with the newly found 'Thank-God' hold, a stretch round the overhang on the left enabled a small undercut hand-hold to be used by the left hand for a pull round the corner and up to a neat little ledge just to the left and above the bottom of the overhang.

After a rest here, on what was a reasonable stance, it became obvious that there were no belays in the vicinity. However, on the right along the side of the overhang an obvious layback crack of fifteen odd feet led to the possibility of a runner behind a rather shaky flake. On return to the ledge the route became only too obvious! The ledge itself was on top of an overhang; there was an overhanging wall on the right; and directly above were what the guide-book terms 'the obvious over-hangs of Bloody Slab.' The only way led diagonally upwards and across the smooth and exposed slab to the left.   Fifteen feet away to the left was a thin vertical grassy crack and between this and the ledge the only holds were very tiny vertical ribs; in effect the ideal place for a horizontal rappel.   This was done by using the rope through the runner on the shaky flake which allowed a precarious crab-like movement to be made across into the grassy crack.

From this point on the upper slab proper it was possible to climb diagonally up to the left on tiny finger- and toe-holds with the occasional use of a clump of grass growing in thin vertical cracks.   At one stage when embracing such a strip of grass with hands and feet the top portion came away from the crack and started to peel off, rolling down from the top like a thin green carpet.   With a seventy-foot lead-out from the last runner—the shaky flake—the situation was critical and the piton-hammer was rapidly brought into use to cut off the detached part of the clump before the whole thing rolled right off. Quick movement off the grass was of course quite impossible owing to the thin and delicate nature of the climb.   On the upper portion of the slab there was no trace of any real hold so all movements had to be carefully studied in order to maintain three good points of contact with the rock while looking for, or making, the next move.

Shifting carefully off the grass, movement could again be made diagonally upward to the left on very tiny rugosities until another large loose flake was reached.   This appeared to be resting on a useful little ledge, so bridged on very small toe-holds, it proved quite a surprise when a tentative pull removed the whole issue—all twenty odd pounds of it!   This presented an awkward problem, more so in view of the fact that I was holding on it!   One could, of course, hold the flake against the rock, but not for long, and it was too heavy to throw clear without falling off.   Throwing would of course also remove two very good handholds—and if I dropped it—well my feet were just below.   Ted and Brian down below could not have known what was going on until, with a little push to the left, I half-dropped, half-threw it just clear of my left foot to slither noisily down the slab and over the overhang to crash, after a moment's silence, to the screes below.

Just to complete the picture, the groove from which the flake had come was rounded top and bottom with no trace of the hoped-for hold. Almost desperate examination of the rock, however, revealed a tiny flake the top of which was knocked off with the hammer to produce a neat little quarter-inch ledge.   Using this as a finger-hold a move could again be made across and up to another grassy strip. Proceeding super-carefully up this (a ninety-foot lead-out from the shaky flake

11(b). Ron Moseley on Direct Start, Brant. The technique of bridging

Photo by R. Moseley

11(a). Joe Brown on White Slab, Clogwyn du'r Arddu

runner), it again became possible to move on to the more rugose left edge of the slab which led up to a good grassy ledge. . . .

Nobody proved able to second this pitch, and John had to unrope and finish the climb on his own.

But giving all credit due to others for great achievements, Brown and Whillans were undoubtedly the driving force behind the new age in climbing. It was their achievement to bring to the great cliffs of Wales a standard of climbing hitherto reserved for the outcrops: but this advance has been more than merely one of technique. Their eye for a route has been combined with a refusal to be deterred by the appearance of anything, or by any weather conditions. They possess the ability to relax and rest in positions where the average good climber is clinging on desperately trying to move fast before he falls off; indeed Whillans has been heard to speak of relaxing into a layback position. Both of them climb fast on the average, giving an impression of unlimited suppleness and energy, and Whillans has a particular hankering for overhangs. For these reasons, their climbs are not merely of exceptional difficulty, but are unexcelled for position and architecture, that touchstone of a great climb. The purely climbing qualities of these men are combined with an unusually quick and cunning eye for protection. It will be appreciated what force of character and nervous energy are required to lift climbing into a new sphere, to select and carry out climbs of this order: which makes it all the more remarkable to reflect that in Brown's and Whillans's case this was done in their late teens and early twenties. Only now, after a lapse of four years, have a few climbers begun slowly and cautiously to repeat their climbs. It is noticeable that many of these are still in or close to their legal minority, and that the second best build for climbing is perhaps also becoming discernible, for of these youngsters those who do not share the mighty atom physique of the protagonists are mostly long and light and wiry, with powerful fingers. Probably in future all really front-rank rock climbers will be young. This is bound to modify the guide-book position drastically, for those who are doing the new climbs may be too youthful to write the books, and those who are able to write them may no longer be able to do the climbs.

It will be noted that in all cases I have stressed finger strength. This has not happened by accident. It was once fashionable and true to say that it was not necessary to be strong to be a good climber provided one had the necessary balance and technique and determination. This is no longer so: and while there will no doubt be occasional exceptions, the fact must be faced by future climbers that unless they approximate in build to one of the two specifications mentioned above they have little hope of coming within reaching distance of the top standard of their time—and such exceptions as there may be will be due to unusual strength, giving parity in the all-important power-to-weight ratio. Foot-work, technique, determination, and a cool head remain as important as ever, and form the spring-board from which the would-be tiger must take off, but they are not enough in themselves, for a very good reason. This is that all the balance technique in the world is not going to suffice you when climbing an overhang. What has happened is that the average angle of the crux pitches of new climbs has progressively steepened until now it is well past the vertical. At the same time they have become more and more sustained so that both strength and stamina are necessary to overcome them. For balance technique the climber of the 1950's has substituted out-of-balance technique. He has learnt a host of tricks and knacks, presses, sideways leans, oppositions, jams of all sorts, sprags and so on, which enable him to conserve his energy and confidence on overhangs; yet it may be true that brute force and ignorance can achieve more on this type of climb than they could in the more classical style, and this may explain why some very ungraceful-looking and inexperienced climbers sometimes pull off remarkable things. A thrusting approach is no less essential than strong fingers. To acquire all these things training is a *sine qua non*. The fact may be repugnant to some, but there it is: it is no longer enough to be a rock-gymnast, but a highly competent gymnast in training, just as in the rop rank of any other sport nowadays. The best training for climbing is perhaps climbing, and a minimum of one day a week must be aimed at to produce real results. This more or less necessitates quick access to an outcrop, for only on an outcrop can one's physical limits be safely discovered and extended, the thousand and one tricks of the trade be learned, judgment be developed, nerve be tempered, and stamina be acquired. It is stamina, both nervous and physical, that makes the difference between safe and desperate leading on extremely severe rock. And outcrops also give one a chance to develop one other thing.

A few men are born endowed by Nature with rock intelligence. That is, they have only to look at a given piece of rock to see almost at once how to climb it. On steep climbs where the physical strain is extremely high this genius is very valuable, for it permits confident and rapid movement over ground where much hesitation and loss of time would quickly lead to exhaustion and at best retreat, at worst disaster. Anybody possessing this quality will be a good climber; anybody in whom it is joined with the other physical and moral attributes which I have mentioned above will be a great climber. For the vast majority of us, however, who possess it in a much more limited degree, there is quite a good substitute, namely a well-stocked situation memory. Faced with an awkward move on Clogwyn y Grochan we remember a similar combination of holds at Helsby or Froggat and apply the same formula. Obviously to develop this faculty the more one can climb the better, and preferably on a wide variety of rock. This is the other thing that outcrops have to give. Without either rock intelligence or a good situation memory all other fine faculties will be like Samson blind.

Simultaneously with the stirring events just related much exploration at a more reasonable level (and of far more value to the average climber) has been carried on in the Moelwyns, around Tremadoc, on the Rivals, and in the ranges immediately south of Rhyd-ddu. I have already had occasion to mention Tony Moulam as the instigator of this wave. His work has been taken up and continued by that fine climbing team Mike Harris and John Neill, who are joint authors of the forthcoming guide-book to the area. Also prominent at Tremadoc has been Pat Vaughan, and Showell Styles and P. Orkney Work have contributed a number of easier routes here and there. The cliffs in the Moelwyns above Tan y Grisiau are big and of excellent rock. Their frontage is also considerable, but unfortunately they suffer from

the rather unattractive foreground of Tan y Grisiau itself.   But
the climbing on them is good.   Tremadoc is quite different.
The cliffs run in a long line above the road, and are easily accessible.   The scenery is rural and the cliffs look out to sea.   They
are of rather different texture and formation from any others in
Wales, and from the road are not particularly impressive to look
at.   But they are fine to look from, and the climbs on them are
comparable in standard and length with those on the Three
Cliffs.   Craig y Bere on Mynydd Mawr, south of Rhyd-ddu, is
fine and wild both to look at and to look from, but the rock is
rather rotten for comfort, and much the same can be said of Craig
yr Cwm Du on the other side of the mountain.   The mountain
itself is a grand one, however, and the cliffs are worth a visit for
the exciting rock scenery of their jagged ridges.   Y Garn, on the
other side of the valley, has a fine east ridge that deserves to be
climbed more often, and quite a lot of unclimbed rock.   In
Cwm Dulyn above Nantlle, too, are large untouched faces.
Cwm Silyn is of course an established classic and should need no
introduction: its views and its climbs and its unclimbed rock are
among the best in Wales, yet comparatively few climbers ever go
there.   And long climbs of over seven hundred feet are now being
found in the Rivals.   Farther south again are other relatively
unexplored ranges.   The scope is endless.   Too few mountaineers ever swerve from the arterial highways of Idwal and Tryfan
and the Three Cliffs to take advantage of the wealth of climbing in
this area, but perhaps that is a good thing.   Even though the
more fashionable mountain-sides swarm like ant-hills and rever-
berate with traffic and inharmonious voices (though they were
once so secret) those who seek solitude to climb will probably for
some years yet be able to pass a summer's day in these southern
ranges without too close sight or sound of other humans.   For
beauty they are not surpassed in Arvon, and often one can climb
there in sunshine and watch the serried rain clouds towering
beyond Snowdon and up Llanberis.   For the last year or two the
region has become a preferred one for those who seek new climbs
without aspiring quite to the dizzy technical heights that have
become the element of the explorer on du'r Arddu and the slopes
of the Glyders, and it is likely to remain so for some time.   Some

good things are periodically found in the Carnedds, which are far from being fully exploited. G. Francis and the late A. Kopczynski found another fine route on Llech Ddu in 1953, and the possibility remains for more.

The year 1954 saw new names emerge. Hugh Banner, Chris Bonnington, and Peter Biven all added new routes to the Llanberis cliffs as well as repeating some of the Rock and Ice climbs there and on Cloggy. Brown and Whillans kept up the good work by climbing the Broad Walk on Clogwyn y Grochan, a line which had attracted notice for years. They found more openings on Craig Ddu, the lowest and most neglected of the Three Cliffs. These, with Banner's Cornix and Ochre Grooves, Bonnington's Griffon, and new girdles of Wastad and Grochan, not to mention literally dozens of variations more or less worthy, made it seem that climbing in the valley had reached finality: yet the following year N'gombo was added to the Grochan and more to Craig Ddu. A still more ferocious finish was given to the Erosion Grooves by Whillans. More routes were found on Craig Rhaiadr by Roscoe, and the Nose of Dinas Mot yielded the Link to Brown and the Cross-tie, a sort of counter-diagonal, to Banner. The upper wing of the cliff, till then surmounted only by Edwards's delectable Slow Ledge, gave another climb.

The weather was exceptional that year in Britain. Returning soaked and shivering from some Alpine climb, which frustration had caused one to assault despite the gloomy portents, one was greeted by letters still warm with news of sun-baked slabs in Wales, Cloggy the only place cool enough to climb on. The possible lines were becoming few on Cloggy. There was, and is, quite a lot of unclimbed rock on the Far East Buttress, but on the main crag the possibilities were diminishing. In a couple of attempts on the White Slab which were foiled by the weather, Brown had succeeded in forcing a new entry to the West Buttress, and getting a considerable way up the slab. The problem of finding routes on this buttress has always been very much the problem of finding entries. The base of the cliff is heavily undercut. The overhangs are peculiarly sharp, smooth, and continuous. Prior to the ascent of the Red Slab, all the climbs had either circumvented these overhangs by starting, like

Linnell's Leap on the Narrow Slab, above the Middle Rock, and traversing above them, or they had funnelled across the delicate little grace of undercut slablet which prefaces the feast of the Great Slab.   The Red and Carpet Slabs found their own way on, but they were up at the other end.   The entry to White Slab had been plain for all to see, but people had been trying it for years in vain—indeed there were rumours of great men tumbling in undignified attitudes at the foot of it.   So that with Brown's ascent, the last of the entries seemed to have been solved.   It had occurred to many that there was lots of room between Central Rib and Red Slab, but unfortunately this was the very point at which the initial overhangs were at their most intimidating.   It came as rather a shock to hear that Whillans, having profited from the fine weather to get into training with second ascents of Cenotaph Corner, the Grooves, and the new East Buttress routes, had succeeded in forcing a way up these overhangs and up the cliff above, which entailed at one point a run-out of 180 feet.   Fortunately nowadays most explorers carry two or three hundred feet of nylon, and 150 feet is becoming a standard length.   He has not yet been prevailed upon to give this route a name, so it is generally referred to as 'the route to the left of the Bloody Slab.'   Since the cliff already has a 'Pigott's' and a 'Longland's,' why not a 'Whillans's Route'?[1]   The adoption of the name would be a graceful solution to the problem.   When Brown returned from Kangchenjunga, he and Whillans made a new and even for them unusually ferocious route on the Pinnacle Face up the undercut square corner on the left (led by Whillans) on which one is informed that the overhang is climbed by laybacking (or would it be laying back?) on the undercut finger-holds.   They followed this up with yet another exceptional route near the left end of the Far East.

After so much trying and now that most other attractions were eliminated, it was evident that the White Slab would have to go sooner or later, and in the spring of 1956 Moseley was the successful candidate, starting from Linnell's Leap.   A day or so later it was repeated, with Brown's original direct start, by Whillans. This was perhaps the last great natural line on the West, and must

[1] This route has now been named Slanting Slab.

be one of the hardest. The writer remembers the uneasiness of doing the delicate traverse of Linnell's Leap with Brown cheerfully perched on what appeared to be nothing and complaining of a bilious attack some forty feet above, on the occasion of one of the explorations. It was remarkable how the sight of all this going on a few feet away made the holds on our own climb seem unsportingly large, but on inquiry we were told that so far it was only 'very mild Extreme,' and that he was climbing like a ninny that day. After White Slab attention turned to the main unsolved problem of the East, and before this book is published it seems possible that No-vember will have succumbed.[1] After this it is likely that another jump in standard will be required to produce new routes on the main buttresses. The obvious lines will nearly all have gone; yet, as Moulam has remarked, new routes seem to be in the eye of the beholder.

The Cambridge climbers, led chiefly by Bob Downes and John Turner, have repeated a number of the new climbs during 1955 and 1956; and the Wallasey parties led by Tony Stead have been equally active. Certain climbers have begun to make artificial climbs here and there, a practice which seems difficult to condone in Wales, more particularly when some of them have been repeated by other climbers without pitons. Such climbs are useful as practice for Alpine work when put up legitimately in limestone in Derbyshire, Yorkshire, and elsewhere; but seem retrograde in Wales or Cumberland or on gritstone, where the habit until now, on finding a passage one could not surmount without using more than one or two pegs, has been to leave it for a better man or to go away and learn to climb better oneself. Getting up rock of XS standard by the immoderate use of pegs does not mean that one has become an XS leader, merely that one has brought the climb down to one's own standard, whatever that may be. This is not intended as a diatribe against pitons, but as a suggestion that, in Wales, for the good of Welsh climbing (and one's own), one has no right to make artificial pitches until one is capable of doing most if not all of the existing free climbing. Parties which have failed on climbs relatively as easy as the Spectre (for example) should beware of the phrase

[1] It is still holding out (November 1956).

'A2.'   Among north country parties the habit has been growing of begging the question by use of inserted chock-stones and threaded slings.   While this is undoubtedly more difficult and often more dangerous than using pegs and stirrups, one is unable to see in what it differs morally, or on what ground chock-stone users are able to criticize peg users—more especially when such aid is often left unacknowledged in subsequent descriptions. This last practice can only be considered dishonest.

Dinas Cromlech (Plate 8), perhaps the finest of the Three Cliffs, was finally girdled by Brown and Whillans at Easter 1956, an expedition which demanded two days (one remembers that the East Buttress girdle on Cloggy took six and a half hours).   The photographs taken on the climb speak for themselves.   Shortly afterwards Moseley, having repeated Cenotaph Corner, put a most unlikely looking route on its left wall (as you look at it). It seems probable again that most of what can be done of importance on the Three Cliffs has now been accomplished—though one or two challenges remain on Dinas Cromlech and opposite on Cyrn Las.   Cloggy too, Elidir Fawr, Cwm Silyn, Cwm Dulyn —something remains.

But the most beautiful lines to explore are now in Scotland and Ireland.   The Snowdon hills are, for now, married to man. There is still personal discovery, the joy of personal conquest— but they are grown up now, it is too late for illusion, the imagination must play on known and loved fact, not on what may be. Only when the men are all gone the mist will settle again, and in the morning it will be as young as ever it was.

The knowledge of what the Rock and Ice Club explorers are capable of if called upon has made the mental barrier to the repetition of their climbs comparable to (or in some cases almost greater than) that of a first ascent.   Year by year more of them are repeated by more people—still in general the easier ones; it is possible at present to make a name as a climber simply by repeating their easier routes—and one discovers that these are no harder than the hardest of the old.   But the bigger ones brook no attempt at denigration.   They are as far ahead of their time as the most marked advances of the past, they mark a definite jump forward—I use the word jump on purpose, after reflection—and

12(b). Joe Brown and Don Whillans

12(a). John Streetly on the first ascent, Red Slab, Clogwyn du'r Arddu

to say this is to compliment rather than depreciate the deeds of earlier climbers.   One is also in a position to state that in difficulty of free climbing they are a standard or more in front of anything to be found in the Alps at the present time.   One can say of Brown and Whillans, as Kretschmer said of Kirkus and Edwards (one might add Harding, Herford, Archer Thomson, the Abrahams, and other great names of the past), that 'not only did they between them make many more first ascents and discoveries than did all the other climbers together, during the whole period, but . . . their direct influence has been, and is, felt by all outstanding rock climbers of recent times.'

What of the future?   To speculate is rash but irresistible. There is no doubt that the hills will become more and more crowded as the years go by.   The standard of rock climbing will continue to rise, and eventually it is bound to take another jump forward.   Exploration will be pushed into increasingly remote cliffs and ranges, and it seems likely that further exploitation of cliffs already as worked out as those in Llanberis will become increasingly artificial both in the means employed and in the ends attained.   Perhaps it is not an enticing prospect, but the mountains at least will be the same, and each generation will find its own way and its own good times upon them.   The valleys may be changed beyond recognition, whether for better or worse, by the various hydro-electric schemes now afoot.   To predict more would be foolish.

We have brought our survey of what may legitimately be called modern climbing in 1956 to a close.   New faces are constantly appearing, new names are bruited about, and old ones disappear. New soon changes to old, and last year's wonder will soon be ancient history, to be referred to with a smile: 'Those old boys certainly did some remarkable things, considering they only had pitons and nylon rope.'   If during our course we have seemed to lose sight of the hills among a crowd of knots, karabiners, gym shoes, nylon slings, and the ephemeral names of men, it is only because that has been our subject for now.   The mountains have been there all the time in their patience.   It is true to-day that the crowds that circulate on the summits are largely not the crowds that clutter the more accessible cliffs, but that does not mean that appreciation is the prerogative of one species.   Each brings and takes away in his own kind.   Rock and turf is only rock and turf, however the changing expressions of sun and cloud may suggest mood on those bald brows, and they remain equally indifferent to the litter-hound, the dreamer, or the seeker of reputation.   Climb up the great slab of Cwm Silyn or walk over y Foel Grach any evening of the year out of the August Saturdays, and whether the year is 1850 or 1950 or 2050 you will not be able to tell from the silence that encircles you, the sun going down into the ocean, or the moss and stones deadening to grey under your feet.

IV

The Writer in Snowdonia

by

WILFRID NOYCE

The Writer in Snowdonia

My prelude must be an apology to the Welsh. Snowdon, or rather Eryri, is their mountain, home of their Awen (Muse) and sacred to them as was Parnassus to the Greeks. Here am I, a Sassenach with scarcely a word of Welsh in my quiver, doomed to look at it with Sassenach eye and to write of it, worse still, with a Sassenach pen. Moreover, as I have read of it in English, my account is bound to be of Snowdon in *English* rather than Welsh literature: the way in which the attitude to life and indeed the philosophy of some of my countrymen was affected by what they experienced here, since the days when Giraldus Cambrensis, of his tour in 1188, wrote: 'I must not pass over in silence the mountains called by the Welsh Eryri, but by the British Snowdon, or Mountains of Snow, which . . . seem to rear their lofty summits even to the clouds.'

I apologize therefore for the briefness of my quotations from the Welsh poets, on the grounds that to record all development even in the English writing about Snowdon over these years would demand a volume of its own; and I am limited for space. What a development it is! How far from peaceful Giraldus are passages, say, in the new rock-climbing guide-books, such as the following: 'Start the overhang by bridging, using holds in the crack: there is a piton above on the right which gives both protection and direct aid. The climbing at this point and above is exceptionally severe, strenuous and in a very exposed position. Above the overhang the crack narrows and after one good hand-jam the pull-out is made on small finger-holds.' [1]

Since I have not the space, and scarcely the knowledge, for the English writers, how much at sea would I be with the Welsh poets in detail, since once embarked on that ocean there would be no

[1] *Climbers' Club Guide to Llanberis,* by P. R. J. Harding, 1950. The Ivy Sepulchre.

hope of reaching port at all. 'There is no mountain or hill within its [Wales's] bounds which has been left unsung by the bards who have sprung in such numbers from its soil.' So L. J. Roberts wrote,[1] and to make matters worse the translations are of little help. Dante never moved me till I knew him in Italian, nor Homer, divorced from the Greek. I am unable to appreciate Borrow's claim that Welsh poetry stands as high as or higher than any; certainly not when it trips in doggerel couplets from the Borrovian tongue. Better therefore to be honest in admission and frank in excuse; acknowledging as I pass that the names of Rhys and Iolo Goch, of Twm wr Nant and Huw Morris, of the great Dafydd ap Gwilym and Goronwy Owen, may sound depths more profound than anything that I shall cite as worthy of admiration.

Lastly, another feature of this chapter needs to be mentioned. I have devoted more space to, indeed sometimes almost reviewed, the more modern writing. The reasons for this are threefold. First, this book treats mainly of mountaineering, and mountaineering literature is modern literature. Secondly, the gap left by *The Mountains of Snowdonia* is in recent rather than classical literature. Finally, my hope is to encourage others, be they bardic or prosaic, to take the pen and write of Snowdon; which they will be more encouraged to do by the example of their contemporaries than by that of Dr Johnson or of Twm wr Nant.

2

The early story of Snowdon in literature is tinged, indeed dyed, with romance. It is a tint that has coloured the mountain ever since, and distinguished it from any other in Britain. Who that has passed Bwlch y Saethau on a frosty winter's afternoon does not seem to hear the clash of King Arthur's arms? But for me the story begins on the mound of Dinas Emrys, one and a half

---

[1] 'Snowdon in Welsh Poetry,' *The Mountains of Snowdonia*, 1925. See also the bibliography at the end of this book. This shows a little learning to be as dangerous a thing in this as in other fields. I am contenting myself with the passing impression.

miles up the Nant Gwynant valley from Beddgelert: the strong-hold built by the British King Vortigern, at a time when he had irritated his own subjects by treating with the Saxon invaders, and was now in danger at Saxon hands after all. Dinas Emrys means quite simply the fortress of Ambrosius, for the building of this fort is associated with the arrival on the scene of the 'marvellous boy' Ambrosius Merlinus, whom we know as Merlin. The legend of the Welsh poets has it that he proved his identity miraculously, as well as his power of prophecy, and advised the king to remove his castle to Dinas Emrys; which advice the king took. And it is the Arthurian legend here begun which has stirred the tongues of poets as tunefully as any other in British history.

The appearance of Merlin, which has some affinities, in a different context, with the selection of the Dalai Lama, is des-cribed in the *Historia Britannorum*, a Latin chronicle that grew up in the seventh and eighth centuries.[1] In so far as it concerns Wales, the story is a mighty vindication of the Welsh side in the struggle between Saxon and Briton; a struggle still bitterly present to many minds as late as the mid-nineteenth century, and of which there are rumblings to this day.

Merlin is the greatest of the Snowdonian figures, but there are others to be found in stories of the *Mabinogion*, compiled from the Red Book of Hergest and translated by Lady Charlotte Guest in the nineteenth century. In this compilation the Arthurian heroes are found fighting and suffering over the Welsh hills; but the topography is too vague for any of their deeds to be pin-pointed. Arvon, or Caernarvon, is fairly clear, the place to which the emperor was directed in dream by the peaks of Snowdon. Clear also to any mountaineer is the last battle, after which Bwlch y Saethau between y Wyddfa and Lliwedd was named; and after which, too, the warriors retired to the cave in the 'Slanting' Gully on Lliwedd,[2] there to sleep until they should be summoned again. I do not know where the further tale springs from, that a shep-herd, searching for his sheep, once entered the cave and hit his

---

[1] See *The Mountains of Snowdonia*, 2nd ed., p. 214 et seq.
[2] The great gully slanting from the right on the West Peak. First climbed 1897.

head on a bell.   This clanged so loud that it awoke the sleepers, who sprang to their feet thinking that the day of their summoning had come.   The poor shepherd was never the same man again.

For a picture of Arthur as the sturdy Welsh chieftain repelling Saxons, rather than the heroic twelfth-century sovereign of Geoffrey of Monmouth, see a short essay by G. H. P. Beames in *Dawn Rides*.   The question is also raised; where did he live? Bala has been suggested, with a thought of Spenser:

> His dwelling is low in a valley greene
> Under the fort of Ranrau mossy hore,
> From whence the River Dee as silver cleene
> His tombling billows rolls with gentle rore.

And it is of interest that Tennyson stayed at Bala while writing Arthurian poetry; while Sir Bedivere is quoted as being buried in the 'woody steep of Tryfan.'

The latest conclusion of scholars, therefore, seems to be that Arthur was a Romano-Briton chief (not a king at all) who led the armies to repulse the Saxon in the sixth century.   But he operated throughout the north and west,[1] not tied to a locality.

I like the story of the shepherd because it is a reminder that the shepherds were plying their trade unnoticed alongside the heroes and bards; just as they must have been making ascents of Snowdon, before ever one was written down on a page likely to come before our eyes.   They must have seen their home used as fortress and asylum.   To us they appear mainly in the faintly fancy dress of the eighteenth- and nineteenth-century writers, Peacock for instance and Thomas Gray.   The poet-seer of *The Bard* watches, as the shepherds must have watched, the Saxons winding their way down towards Caernarvon; and he curses them to their doom before the hosts of Arthur:

> But oh! what solemn scenes on Snowdon's height
>   Descending slow their glitt'ring skirts unroll!
> Visions of glory, spare my aching sight,
>   Ye unborn Ages, crowd not on my soul!
> No more our long-lost Arthur we bewail.
> All hail ye genuine Kings, Britannia's Issue, hail!

[1] See Dayrell Reid, *The Battle for Britain in the Fifth Century*.   His conclusions are disputed however.

I sometimes wonder how much Gray really knew of Arthur's own rock-climbing propensities, already quoted from Malory on page 19.

3

The poets of the Arthurian period, Taliesin and Aneurin for instance, seem, like the Greeks before them, less concerned with the hills than with the lower fields: pleasant as it would be to imagine, with Peacock, that Taliesin learned his lore upon Eryri, and that it was a Snowdon sou'wester that he experienced when he conceived his 'Ode to the Wind.'[1]

> It comes from the four quarters
> It will not be advised,
> It will not be without advice.
> It commences its journey
> Above the marble rock.
> It is sonorous, it is dumb,
> It is mild,
> It is strong, it is bold. . . .

But the tale is of fights rather than of fells, of carousals rather than of crags; until, as the centuries wear on, the picture of Arthur's company grows dimmer, transfigured by the mist of legend.   Like the Alps, these mountains lost their hold as places of resort, or even of war, places where men slept and moved and where fortresses were built.   But they remained, as did also the Alps, the home of other and more awesome denizens, of monstrous and deformed fish, and—most famous of all—of the afanc. George Borrow, musing by a wayside pool as he walked from Ffestiniog to Bala, decided that this name must imply something terrible in its possessor; that the original afanc must have been fiercely crocodilian, even if later the harmless tribe of beavers took over the title.   The historicity of afancs does not concern us.   All we need to know is that the poetic imagination of writers filled the lakes and ponds with these monsters.   The biggest of all disappeared into Llyn Idwal and gave its name to the

[1] Translated in Elizabeth A. Sharp's *Lyra Celtica*, 1896.

Nant Ffrancon. Another is recorded as being dragged all the way from its home, across the mountains of Dolwyddelan, by two oxen. It was cast into Glaslyn, where to the relief of all it disappeared. One of the oxen's eyes fell out with the effort and formed a tarn. The afanc had the last word:

> Had it not been for the oxen pulling
> The afanc never had left the pool.

Because of this new inhabitant Glaslyn is now bottomless, never freezes in winter (I have walked across it, but the legend remains), no birds will fly over it, and it is shunned by all ordinary fish.[1]

Llyn du'r Arddu is another lake that preserves legends of the same type as those studiously noted by the Swiss travellers. This time the fairy is friendlier, and at times even has intercourse with humans. The dogged persistence of these Snowdon legends even into the nineteenth century is shown by an extract from a Welsh magazine, the *Greal*, as late as 1805:

There is a lake in the mountains of Snowdon, called Dulyn, in a rugged valley, encircled by high steep rocks. This lake is extremely black, and its fish are deformed and unsightly, having large heads and small bodies. No wild swans are ever seen alighting upon it (such as are on the other lakes of Snowdon), nor any other bird whatever. And there is a causeway of stones leading into this lake, and if anyone goes along this causeway, even when it is hot sunshine, and throws water so as to wet the furthest stone, which is called the Red Altar [yr Allawr Goch], it is a chance if it do not rain before night. Witness T. Prys, of Plas Iolyn, and Sion Davydd, of Rhiwlas, in Llan Silin [*sic*].[2]

4

Thus the hold of the dragons on Snowdonia remained strong; magic fish peopled its pools and fairies walked its shores[3] long after the Age of Reason had left every other land bare and

---

[1] *Celtic Folklore*, p. 473. See also Sir John Lloyd's article, 'The Mountains in Legend and History,' *The Mountains of Snowdonia*, p. 3 et seq.

[2] This belief is mentioned in *The Golden Bough* by Sir James Frazer. Abridged edition, p. 76.

[3] The fairies of Llyn Crwrion are the most charming.

unbeautiful, ready to be invaded by those new and eccentric visitors, the artist, the author, and the climber.

Advancing beyond the enchanted Middle Ages we cannot help casting a glance at that disastrous hero, Owen Glyndwr or Glendower (1359–1415). This is no history, no place to assess how far Glendower was a scourge to his own country. Certainly the Welsh would have been more prosperous had he never lived. But the same is true of many a hero, from Achilles onward. The nation's pride and legend would be correspondingly poorer. Not unnaturally, the story here is in Welsh rather than English, and I must leave those competent to read it among the pages of Iolo Goch, who has sung his praises loud enough. Another great contemporary poet, Rhys Goch Eryri (*fl.* 1400), was born at Ffestiniog and used to compose on a seat forming part of a Druid circle there; which stone Borrow tried but failed to identify.

> Honour doth still the stone adorn
> In Snowdon's height where I was born.

and

> My British privilege I claim
> Ungrudged of all my fame:
> And Snowdon keeps the far-famed stone,
> Which rightfully this day I own.

Rhys Goch is a poet of whom a fair impression may be gained in *Lyra Celtica*. His main theme is passionate invective against the brutal English.

With Owen Glendower English literature, apart from Shakespeare in *Henry IV*, Part I, has missed a golden opportunity. There is room for more than the firebrand. The rocks and valleys still smell of his melodramatic appearances and disappearances; I cannot pass Harlech Castle without thinking of the sieges which inspired 'The March,' nor Moel Hebog without looking up at the black slit in Moel yr Ogof and thinking, what a possibility for the theatre here! To anyone who has scrambled along the ledge into the cave, with its impressive drop down the limestone cliff below, his ghost is still there, as he lay shivering and staring into the mist, wondering whether hunger or the English lances were the more hateful, reflecting, in the later years,

on the moments of glory that had held the hated Grey prisoner in
Dolbadarn Castle, only a few miles away.   Those moments of
glory had been good.   To think that Grey had been squeezed so
tightly that the king was obliged to appoint a special commission
to collect enormous ransom money. . . .   And now he was
starving, and the mist was cold.   Suddenly the clatter of foot-
steps. . . .

Dolbadarn, near the shores of Llanberis lake, was itself a
romantic stronghold.   Here Owen Goch, brother of Llewelyn
and Dafydd, spent over twenty years, for very good reason.
Here Glendower himself must have been imprisoned more than
once.   But we must pass by these, to take off an apologetic hat
for a moment to Dafydd ap Gwilym (1340–c. 1400), perhaps the
greatest of all the Welsh poets, for being unable to quote from
him directly on the mountain theme.   *The Fox* in translation
must suffice:

> The wretch my starry bird who slew,
> Beast of the flameless ember hue,
> Assassin, glutton of the night,
> Mixed of all creatures that defile,
> Land-lobster, fugitive of light,
> Thou coward mountain crocodile;
> With down-cast eyes and ragged tail,
> That haunt'st the hollow rocks,
> Thief, ever ready to assail
> The undefended flocks,
> Thy brass-hued breast and tattered locks
> Shall not protect thee from the hound,
> When with unbaffled eye he mocks
> Thy mazy fortress underground,
> Whilst o'er my peacock's shattered plumes shall shine
> A pretty bower of fairy eglantine.
>
> [Elizabeth A. Sharp's translation.]

The age of Elizabeth Tudor brings new travellers, who start
staring at these wonders with eyes that will create a new literary
approach.

5

Already, emerging from the heroic ages, we must note briefly John Leland, whose *Itinerary in Wales* (1536–9) is the first book seriously to note the hills as geographical entities, separate and apart.   Meanwhile, more divertingly, here is Ben Jonson at about the same time:

Jenkin: Why law you now, iss not Penmaenmawr and Craig-Eriri as good sound as Adlas, every whit of him?
Evan: 'Iss call'd the British Alpes, Craig-Eriri, a very sufficiaunt hills.

A more important document is the *Britannia* of William Camden, a geographical description written in Latin and appearing in 1586.   We shall see this again in the work of Edward Llwyd, who translated the section on Wales.   Camden must have been a remarkable person, and his influence was enormous. When, about 1610, John Speed began to publish maps with descriptions in English, these were largely a paraphrase of Camden, whose writing was thus widely quoted.   Here he is on Snowdon: 'These mountains may not unfitly be termed the British Alps, as being the most vaste of all Britain . . . all of them towering up into the aire, and round encompassing one farre higher than alle the rest, peculiarly called Snowdon-Hill . . . for all the year long these lye mantelled over with snow hard crusted together.' It was in 1639 that the botanist, Thomas Johnson, began to write in a more seriously mountaineering vein, with his account of an ascent of Snowdon in search of plants.

. . . we betook ourselves to our British Alps.   The highest of these is called Snowdon by the English and Widhfa by the Britons. . . . [The early start.]   The whole mass of the mountain was veiled in cloud . . . leaving our horses and outer garments, we began to climb the mountain.   The ascent at first is difficult, but after a bit a broad open space is found, but equally sloping, great precipices on the left, and a difficult climb on the right.   Having climbed three miles, we at last gained the highest ridge of the mountain, which was shrouded in thick cloud.   Here the way was very narrow, and climbers are horror-stricken by the rough rocky precipices on either hand and the Stygian marshes, both on this side and that. . . .   [Reaching the summit] we sat down in the midst of the clouds, and first of all we arranged in order the plants we had, at our peril, collected among the rocks and precipices, and then we ate the food we had brought with us.

The early start, the mist, the horror of the precipices, the food at the summit: these were to become the familiar features of countless mountain ascents.   Notice that the purpose is strictly botanical.   Johnson came near the top of Carnedd Llewelyn also, but a faint-hearted guide refused to take the party near the precipices, 'where alone the rarer plants grew,' for fear of eagles.

Johnson and others who followed him wrote after the appearance of Speed's geographical publications, Michael Drayton's *Poly-Olbion* (1612), Ogilby's road maps, etc.[1]   There are two more literary records of the century to be mentioned, partly to show how fearsomely high and remote the mountains on first acquaintance seemed.   In 1652 John Taylor, known as the Water Poet, made a journey through Wales late in life.

> The next day, when the clock strok two and four,
> I mounted Dun [his horse], Dun mounted Penmen Mawre;
> And if I do not take my aime amisse,
> That lofty mountain seems the skies to kisse:
> But there are other hills accounted higher,
> Whose lofty tops I had no mind t'aspire:
> As Snowdon, and the tall Plinnillimon,
> Which I no stomack had to tread upon.[2]

Others were more accurate in measurement; and while in 1682 Caswell put the height of Snowdon at 3,720 feet, and Halley climbed the mountain in 1697 to carry out scientific experiments in 'this horrid spot of hills,' Bishop Gibson was entrusting the Welsh part of his translation of Camden's *Britannia* to Edward Llwyd, keeper of the Ashmolean Museum at Oxford.   Llwyd knew Snowdonia well, and even had a description of the top of

---

[1] See G. A. Lister, 'The Coming of the Mountaineer,' Chapter III, *The Mountains of Snowdonia*.

[2] Penmaenmawr, beloved of Gladstone and scene of the composition of Elgar's *Falstaff*, seemed wild and formidable to early travellers.   Dr Johnson advanced with timidity along the first road, which in 1772 had replaced the bridle-path.

Glyder Fach, at once the goal and frustration of many travellers, since most failed to find it or mixed it up with Glyder Fawr. He also, knowing the mountains as a native, corrected errors in Camden such as that of perpetual snow.

All along here we realize that the main purpose of writing at this time is practical, scientific. It is almost as an afterthought that the good bits come out, such as this one in Llwyd: 'So that, having climbed up one Rock, we come to a valley, and most commonly to a Lake; and passing by that we ascend another, and sometimes a third and a fourth, before we arrive at the highest Peaks.'

He is certainly the most sympathetic writer, until we come, passing very briskly over a barren fifty years at the beginning of the eighteenth century, to the brief but charming description of Lord George Lyttleton. Lyttleton is almost a British Petrarch in this one respect, that he climbed for no other purpose than health and pleasure, with no thought for scientific or any other investigation. His journey of 1756 was undertaken 'so that I may, by this ramble, preserve a stock of health that may last all the winter, and carry me through my parliamentary campaign.' Few parliamentarians are so prudent in these days. Moreover, as concerns us most here, his letters have a turn for descriptive phrase, as for rational conclusion, that makes one wish for more.

On one side was midnight, on the other bright day; the whole extent of the mountain of Snowdon, on our left hand, was wrapped in clouds, from top to bottom; but on the right the sun shone most gloriously over the sea coast of Caernarvon. The hill we stood upon [Hebog] was perfectly clear, the way we came up a pretty easy ascent; but before us was a precipice of many hundred yards [the cliff of Hebog], and below a vale which, though not cultivated, has much savage beauty.

After this we have not long to wait. Very soon figures of more distinctively literary flavour take the field, including the portentous shadow of Dr Johnson.

6

'You will have become quite a mountaineer, by visiting Scotland one year and Wales another.   You must next go to Switzerland.   Cambria will complain, if you do not honour her also with some remarks.'   So Boswell to Johnson, of the latter's visit to Snowdonia in 1774.   But the result is disappointing, particularly if you compare it with the fruits of the journey to the Hebrides.   I had hoped from the Doctor for some further justification of the tenet I elaborated, that the eighteenth century left the mountains a 'Uniformity of Barrenness,' 'reft of their dragons and demons, but not yet the abode of any more substantial form of life.' [1]   The Age of Reason was too solid, purposeful if you like.   The hills had become hindrances to rational progress, since they could not be cultivated and were obvious and ugly barriers to communication.

Yet, surprising as it seems, nobody can call the Doctor unsympathetic, to the scrambler at least, for not only did he boast of his feats in climbing college walls, he wrote of a hill scene thus: 'Its grandeur is tempered with softness; the walker congratulates his own arrival at the place, and is grieved to think that he must ever leave it.   As he looks up to the rocks, his thoughts are elevated; as he turns his eyes on the vallies, he is composed and soothed.'   Anybody who can write that is more than half way to being a mountaineer; and he is quite a mountaineer who can exclaim: 'He that mounts the precipices wonders how he came thither, and doubts how he shall return.   His walk is an adventure, and his departure an escape.   He has not the tranquillity, but the horrors, of solitude; a kind of turbulent pleasure, between fright and admiration.'

But of Wales Dr Johnson has little to say, albeit that little is not unfavourable: 'Wales is so little different from England, that it offers nothing of speculation to the traveller.'   And Boswell records sadly of this journey that 'though it no doubt contributed to his health and amusement [he was with the Thrales] . . . I do not find that he kept any journal or notes of what he saw there. All that I heard him say of it was, that instead of bleak and barren

[1] *Scholar Mountaineers*, p. 15.

mountains, there were green and fertile ones; and that one of the castles of Wales would contain all the castles that he had seen in Scotland.'[1] But his only excursion into the realm of *mountain* castles was a visit to Dolbadarn, 'to which we climbed with great labour: I was breathless and harassed.' In all fairness it must be added that he was now sixty-five years of age.

Johnson may be taken to represent the approach of the prose writers of his age, Bishop Burnet the ecclesiastical, and Gray the poetic. Gray had travelled in the Highlands and Lake District in the 1760's; but he confessed that he went no further than Grange in Borrowdale, for 'the mountains bar all further access.' His *The Bard*, therefore, and other poems on Welsh themes, are literary exercises so far as the scenery goes, inspired by the bardic tradition of Wales and the English medieval ballads. The men of Edward are pictured tramping through what is presumably the Valley of Llanberis. 'Shaggy' are the sides of Snowdon, 'awful' the torrents' voice. The oaks are 'giant' and the caves 'desert.' Thus:

> Such were the sounds that, o'er the crested pride
> Of the first Edward scattered wild dismay,
> As down the steep of Snowdon's shaggy side
> He wound with toilsome march his long array.

The poem is of chief interest as a legend, the legend that Edward I ordered every bard to be put to death, whereupon he and his men were cursed by the poet-seer standing on a wayside rock; and for the evocation of Arthur's avenging return at due season.

> But oh! what solemn scenes on Snowdon's height
> Descending slow their glitt'ring skirts unroll! . . .

This evocation is dramatic, and in fervour poetic. The trappings are tinsel.

So we come back to our travellers for the detailed accounts of Snowdon, since the poets do not give them to us, and the painters, such as the charming William Gilpin, lie outside my present scope. In their case writing was the handmaiden, no more, to their art. In 1770, then, Joseph Cradock published his *Letters from Snowdon*, and in 1777 *An Account of Some of the Most Romantic Parts of*

[1] Boswell, *Life*, Modern Library edition, p. 479 et seq.

North Wales. After a long description (typical of the days when the view was justification for the climb to the summit) of the prospect embracing the Wicklow Hills and Cheshire, he adds the nice remark: 'It is doubted whether there is another circular prospect so extensive in any part of the terraqueous globe.' What is of greater interest in these accounts than the narrative is the vagueness of the geography. More than seventy years after Llwyd's description of the distinctive summit of Glyder Fach, these travellers were still searching vainly for it. Henry Penruddocke Wyndham (1774) 'made a diligent enquiry, through Caernarvonshire, for the Glyder mountain which Gibson has particularly described, and which, from its singularity, I much more wished to have seen than the summits of either Plynlimmon or Snowdon.' But see it he never did.

'Books of travel having been mentioned, Johnson praised Pennant very highly,' Boswell records of the year 1778.[1] The Doctor, arguing against Dr Percy, went so far as to describe Thomas Pennant as 'the best traveller I ever read.' In fact Pennant was the outstanding figure in the writing of the time. It is not fair to think of him only as a writer on natural history, though he was that too. He was an explorer with a flair for putting his scenes convincingly across. His *Journey to Snowdon* (1781) was the first guide-book, and he himself the first mountaineer, of his day.

Difficulties such as the whereabouts of the Glyder's summit were soon cleared up by Pennant's observations. Indeed he made first for that mountain, having approached Capel Curig from the direction of Llanrwst. 'Snowdon and all his sons, Crib Goch, Crib y Distill, Lliwedd, Yr Aran, here burst at once full into view, and make this far the finest approach to our boasted Alps.' His ascent of the Glyder from Pont y Gwryd is well known, in particular the descriptive writing of the summit.

The ascent was very long, steep, and laborious, wet and slippery. . . . Our pains were fully repaid, on attaining the summit. The area was covered with groupes of columnar stones, of vast size, from ten to thirty feet long, lying in all directions . . . the tops are frequently crowned in the strangest manner with other stones, lying on them

[1] Ibid. p. 793.

horizontally. One was about twenty-five feet long and six broad. I climbed up, and on stamping it with my foot felt a strong tremulous motion from end to end. . . . In the midst of a vale far below, rises the singular mountain Trevaen, assuming on this side a pyramidal form, naked and very rugged.

Moses Griffith's sketch of Tryfan captures this feature of its 'end-on' appearance.[1]

The party 'made a most hazardous descent to *Cwm Bochllwyd*, and from thence to Llyn Ogwen'; then walked up to Llyn Idwal, 'a fit place to inspire murderous thoughts, environed with horrible precipices, shading a lake, lodged in its bottom.' Then the fables of Idwal, for it is reputed that no bird can fly over its waters. He noticed, as many did not, the Devil's Kitchen. 'Observe, on the right, a stupendous *roche fendue* or split rock, called *Twll Du*, and *the Devil's Kitchen* . . . on surmounting all my difficulties and taking a little breath, I ventured to look down this dreadful aperture [Plate 7(*b*)], and found its horrors far from being lessened, in my exalted situation.' He climbed on over the top of Glyder Fawr, then dropped down to Nant Peris by way of Llyn y Cwm. A very fair day.

Pennant climbed a number of other mountains, including Carnedd Llewelyn, and is noteworthily the first traveller to value accuracy and care in description. At the top of Snowdon itself he was not lured by sentiment into forgetting to note that: 'The shadow of the mountain was flung many miles, and showed its bicapitated form; the Wyddfa making one, Crib y Distill the other head.' He also recorded with interest that the lower part of his face peeled off with the sun.

The importance of Pennant lies partly in his approach, modern and practical and competent, and besides, I will maintain, readable; partly in that for a long time travellers and guide-book writers based themselves on his work. Thus William Gilpin, in search of the picturesque, failed to reach the summit of Snowdon, and had to content himself with Pennant's account of it. For there now began a series of record-writers: Arthur Aikin (who modelled himself on the recently published, classic *Voyages dans les Alpes* of de Saussure), the Rev. J. Evans, and W. Hutton.

[1] See Plate 1 for his sketch of Nantberis and Crib Goch.

The latter added to his *North Wales* (1803) scenes from local life
that he visited.   There is a *Welch Wedding* [*sic*] in verse.   It begins:

> 'Mong the rocks of Llanberis where foot comes not nigh,
> No eye sees their summit except a bird's eye,
> Nor aught in the prospect appears to the sight
> But water, and mountains, yet they give delight.

As verse it is not far from Joseph Cottle's immortal lines on a hill:

> Still I toil.
> How long and steep and cheerless the ascent!
> It needs the evidence of close deduction
> To know that I shall ever reach the height!

and perhaps fittingly marks the end of the eighteenth century.
What is new, however, is the eagerness to describe and record,
to get inside the life and to see its legends with a friendly eye.

A much more important book is the *Tour round North Wales*
of the Rev. William Bingley (1798, describing two tours), since
Bingley as a climber is famous for the first recorded rock climb in
Wales, the Eastern Terrace of Clogwyn du'r Arddu (Plate 9),
with the Rev. Peter Williams in 1799.   As a writer he has a turn
for the picturesque anecdote, and for giving impressions of
wonder and awe.   The rock climb belongs properly to another
chapter, except in so far as the leader adopts a device used in the
Inferno by Virgil, loosing his belt to help his companion at a
tricky passage.   But here is the top of Tryfan, Adam and Eve:
'My companion stepped from the top of one to that of the other.
I am not easily alarmed by passing among precipices and my head
is, I believe, as steady as that of most persons, but I must confess I
felt my blood chill with horror at an act which seemed to me so
rash.'   And here is Snowdon, after one of the seven routes by
which he climbed it:

> The steep rock of Clogwyn y Garnedd, whose dreadful precipices are,
> some of them, above two hundred yards in perpendicular height, and the
> whole rock, a series of precipices, was an object which first struck one of
> my companions with terror, and he exclaimed, almost involuntarily:
>
> > 'How fearful
> > And dizzy 'tis to cast one's eyes so low!
> > The crows and choughs that wing the midway air
> > Shew scarce so gross as beetles.'

13(*a*) (*above*). Snowdon summit in the early 1870's

13(*b*) (*left*). The top of the P y G track, Snowdon, in winter

(*Photo by J. Gianelli*)

It would indeed be a fascinating study to linger comparing the various accounts of the top of Snowdon, Bingley's with those of the novelists and then, as we advance, with Borrow's. But we must leave Bingley, a botanist, and approach a lion of literature also to be found, at about the same time, on this summit: William Wordsworth.

7

Coleridge, though he did visit Snowdonia, is irritatingly uncommunicative. But Wordsworth, though wedded to the Lake District, had by fortunate accident wandered through Snowdonia in his youth. Our quarry is the last book of *The Prelude*.

> In one of those excursions (may they ne'er
> Fade from remembrance) through the northern tracts
> Of Cambria ranging with a youthful friend,
> I left Bethgelert's huts at couching-time ...

and he climbed Snowdon.

The ascent by night was uneventful to begin with, indeed prosaic. The two friends walked up behind their guide, each lost in his own thoughts. The dog found and harried a hedge-hog on the path. They went on, through the dark. Then suddenly:

> lo! as I looked up,
> The Moon hung naked in a firmament
> Of azure without cloud, and at my feet
> Rested a silent sea of hoary mist.
> A hundred hills their dusky backs up heaved
> All over this still ocean; and beyond,
> Far, far beyond, the solid vapours stretched,
> In headlands, tongues, and promontory shapes,
> Into the main Atlantic.

Wordsworth has done it again. Just when all seemed to be engulfed in flattest prose, he has become the poet, a supreme poet

K

and a prophet of eternal truths seen through natural objects:
Wordsworth poet of Grasmere, forerunner of the Romantics and
pantheistic singer of Good in Nature.   For a few lines, a few
steps further on, the deeper meaning pervades him.

> it appeared to me the type
> Of a majestic intellect, its acts
> And its possessions, what it has and craves,
> What in itself it is, and would become.
> There I beheld the emblem of a mind
> That feeds upon infinity, that broods
> Over the dark abyss.

The last lines are not only Wordsworth at his greatest; they strike
an utterly new note, one never heard before over the ramparts of
Snowdon and only faintly preluded in the trumpetings of
Rousseau across the Channel.   Hitherto the mountains have
been 'an excrescency,' 'horrid spots,' a 'Uniformity of Barrenness,' at best a ramble or a scientific quarry.   Now they are
invested with a new dignity in their own right, in which they are
to stand draped throughout the nineteenth century and even into
our motor-ridden twentieth.   They have received their own
personality, a beauty of curve and contour which holds the eye
entranced and whose meaning penetrates the heart with awe for
the creating and moving power behind them:

> The power which all
> Acknowledge when thus moved, which Nature thus
> To bodily sense exhibits, is the express
> Resemblance of that glorious faculty
> That higher minds bear with them as their own.

And though the development of such a theme lies outside this
essay, since Wordsworth's work was done chiefly in the Lakes,
the first breath whispering of the Romantic hurricane may indeed
have come from Caernarvonshire as surely as from Westmor-
land.   It is a significant breath.   For to return once more
to the mind:

> One function, above all, of such a mind
> Had Nature shadowed there, by putting forth,
> 'Mid circumstances awful and sublime,

> That mutual domination which she loves
> To exert upon the face of outward things,
> So moulded, joined, abstracted, so endowed
> With interchangeable supremacy,
> That men, least sensitive, see, hear, perceive,
> And cannot choose but feel.

That is to say, these greater shapes of mountains and the contortions of wind and sun upon them do thrum into our 'dull brains' chords from the mightier symphony which is sounding eternally in the air around.   And who that has stood upon Snowdon in moonlight does not feel that he too could cast himself down before a greater presence?   If he cannot worship Wordsworth's God, he may bend the knee before Leslie Stephen's idol; but at any rate, since Wordsworth's day, it will be before a being too great for everyday comprehension, and yet intimately associated with the everyday sensations of us all.

8

It is sad that I cannot follow up this thought in the years that immediately follow.   De Quincey, who might have given literature of another style than Wordsworth's, is annoyingly reticent about the adventures of his youth in Wales.   Keats visited the Lakes, climbed Skiddaw, and left his memory upon the Highlands, but he omitted Snowdonia.   Southey wrote an epic, *Madoc in Wales*,[1] too pedestrian to be quoted as poetry (though references to Snowdon abound), yet not outstanding enough for the *Stuffed Owl* variety of citation.   However in 1812 Shelley stayed at Tanrallt, shortly after his first marriage.   Here he may

---

[1] It is easy to be unjust to Southey.   The story is of the chieftain Madoc, who emigrated west (to America?) after the wars of 1169.   He returned, conveniently by Anglesey, to collect adventurers to join him.   But beside Wordsworth he adds nothing to the picture, though odd lines please mildly:

> The heights of Snowdon on his backward glance
> Hung like a cloud in heaven.

have written parts of *Queen Mab,* those parts in which the creator of *Prometheus Unbound* is most nearly seen.

> Spirit of Nature! here!
> In this interminable wilderness
> Of worlds, at whose immensity
> Even soaring fancy staggers,
> Here is thy fitting temple.

And there may be a recollection of storm across the hills:

> And where the burning wheels
> Eddied above the mountain's loftiest peak
> Was traced a line of lightning.
> Now it flew far above a rock,
> The utmost verge of earth,
> The rival of the Andes, whose dark brow
> Lowered o'er the silver sea.

Only one poem that I know, of the same period, has a specific reference. In the 'Lines on leaving London for Wales' (1812) he writes of the poetic and symbolic Snowdon:

> And he who dares in fancy even to steal
> One draught from Snowdon's ever sacred spring
> Blots out the unholiest rede of worldly witnessing.

Immature; but with youth, the splendour of hope.

At that time the embankment connecting Pren Teg with Portmadoc was a newly wrought wonder, and the embankment across the Traeth was being built. Great storms threatened the whole of a structure that was reclaiming three thousand acres of land. Shelley canvassed for the local movement to raise money to repair the breach, and gave money himself. But alas, apart from this feat and his generosity on that occasion, he was better known for failures to pay butchers' and bakers' bills (albeit smaller than his contributions to the embankment) than for his poetry. He was 'the mad Englishman' wandering over the slopes of Moel Ddu; and once, in a more disreputable connection (for the Welsh sympathize with madness, and have their own poets), he came into trouble for shooting a sheep from motives of humanity. Then he appeared suddenly at the garden window, inexplicably smeared with blood from being attacked, as he said, in the bushes; very soon after which he left.

I like to think that in one of the earliest, undated poems he pictures his rambles on Moel Ddu; as if he had formerly found the personality Wordsworth knew, and then lost it.

> With mountain winds, and babbling springs,
> And mountain seas, that are the voice
> Of these inexplicable things,
> Thou didst hold converse, and rejoice
> When they did answer thee; but they
> Cast, like a worthless boon, thy love away.

And in the same poem:

> Wherefore didst thou build thy hope
> On the false earth's inconstancy?

It is interesting that four years later he had recovered faith, and was writing, after seeing Mont Blanc:

> Thou hast a voice, great Mountain, to repeal
> Large codes of fraud and woe.

Perhaps it was the Portmadoc or *Queen Mab* sentiment that reappeared in the *Euganean Hills* and *Prometheus Unbound*.

The Portmadoc embankment is connected with another name as friendly to Wales as to Shelley. For Thomas Love Peacock saw it finished (1815) and must have been one of the first to record an impression of the new prospect:

Vast rocks and precipices, intersected with little torrents, formed the barrier on the left; on the right, the triple summit of Moelwyn reared its majestic boundary; in the depth was that sea of mountains, the wild and stormy outline of the Snowdonian chain, with the great Wyddfa towering in the midst. The mountain frame remains unchanged, unchangeable; but the liquid mirror it enclosed is gone.

That is *Headlong Hall*. But in *The Misfortunes of Elphin* Peacock made the serious experiment of introducing Welsh poetry, through a novel, to English readers. Everybody knows the War-song of Dinas Vawr, though most misquote it:

> The mountain sheep are sweeter,
> But the valley sheep are fatter
> We therefore deemed it meeter
> To carry off the latter.

> We made an expedition;
> We met a host, and quelled it
> We forced a strong position,
> And killed the men who held it. . . .

And so on.   For some reason, absurdly, another rhyme always jingles into my head alongside this, quoted by George Abraham in *Rock Climbing in North Wales*.   It concerns another aspect of Welsh mutton, the inevitable farmhouse dish.

> This dose you'll more or less repeat
> On each successive day,
> Till when you meet a mountain sheep
> You'll turn the other way.

But Peacock had a firmer sympathy with the Welsh than the songs of the splendidly drunken Seithenyn allow.   For the novel is a romantic justification of them, in their excesses as well as their legitimate aspirations.   Here too there is an embankment, the great embankment of Caredigion which Seithenyn, in his drunken oversight, omits to repair over the portion for which he is responsible; hence ruin to the land of Caredigion.   But in this land, meanwhile, one of the great bards of Wales is discovered, a Moses-like baby in a coracle.   His birth, like Merlin's, is unknown.   And he is brought up in the recesses of Snowdon: 'Taliesin, worshipping Nature in her wildest solitudes, often strayed away for days from the dwellings of Elphin, and penetrated the recesses of Eryri, where one especial spot on the shores of Lake Ceirionydd became the favourite haunt of his youth.   In these lonely recesses he became familiar with the Druids.'   But there is no more.   There is no evidence that the Peacockian, any more than the historical Taliesin, found in these hills anything but a wild meeting-place with the Druids and an eminence from which he could look down on the inhabited plain below.   For at that time, says Peacock in his lengthy account of the regime, Christianity was in conflict with Druidism.   The Druids held the hills, the Christians did battle upon the plains.

There are, besides this, very pleasant vignettes in the book. Taliesin loves Melanghel, daughter of King Elphin, who has been captured by Maelgon Gwyneth:

One day, the ardour of the chase having carried them far beyond their ordinary bounds, they stood together on Craig Aderyn, the Rock of Birds, which overlooks the river Dysyni. This rock takes its name from the flock of birds which have made it their dwelling, and which make the air resonant with their multitudinous notes. Around, before and above them rose mountain beyond mountain, soaring above the leafless forests, to lose their heads in mist; beneath them lay the silent river; and along the opening of its narrow valley, they looked to the not-distant sea.

Here, at the instance of Melanghel, Taliesin promises to obtain the release of Elphin and does so, by a journey which leads him to the court of King Arthur himself at Caerleon, in which the gay Seithenyn reappears, now demoted to butler.

Peacock followed the Geoffrey of Monmouth tradition, as was natural. Arthur is the chivalrous knight of a much later date rather than the rough warrior chieftain that he must really have been. But even here, in this most urbane of novelists, we have felt a breath of the rougher mountain air blowing through. Peacock did not take the mountains too seriously; whereas he did seriously satirize people and customs. His chapter on the education of Taliesin is a masterpiece comparable with Gulliver. The court of Arthur is recognizable among courts (though not Welsh courts) in general. And his Snowdonia is a serious attempt at reconstruction.

In the same vein of not totally serious song Peacock's son-in-law George Meredith left his memorial to the Welsh bard Aneurin. I am undecided how far he is being consciously bardic, how far just enjoying himself. He continues the theme of the struggle between Saxon and Welshman, as in these two typical stanzas:

> Here the Briton, there the Saxon,
> > Face to face, three fields apart,
> Thirst for light to lay their thwacks on
> > Each the other with good heart.
> Dry the Saxon sits, 'mid dinful
> > Noise of iron knits his steel:
> Fresh and roaring with a skinful,
> > Britons round the hirlas reel.

Yellow flamed the meady sunset
        Red runs up the flag of morn.
Signal for the British onset
        Hiccups through the British horn.
Down these hillmen pour like cattle
        Sniffing pastures: grim below
Showing eager teeth of battle
        In his spear-heads lies the foe.

The second stanza especially may be worked artistically into the bardic design.

9

But it is sad that the more poetic association heralded by Wordsworth and Shelley had to wait so long for further expression; in fact until the climbers began to lend a new poetry, that of movement.

For the travellers of the earlier nineteenth century follow generally the pattern of the late eighteenth, with the difference that efficient transport and good roads had increased their number. There is Richard Fenton the archaeologist, the Rev. G. J. Freeman, and the Rev. John Parker, whose book *The Passengers* (1831) records a guideless ascent of Snowdon. By this time 'there is no place more public than the higher ground of Eryri during the summer. A procession composed of all those who visit the Welsh Parnassus would indeed be a motley assemblage.' In literature, as in life, pride of place goes to Snowdon. As one anonymous writer testily put it: 'Snowdon is ascended by everyone because it is the highest top; no one seems to ascend the other mountains but the shepherds of the country. Snowdon is the Righi of Wales, with a trifle worse inn at the top.'

Into this scene steps one of the most important figures in the story, a poet too, though not of the most poetic, even if he fancied himself as a rhymster. George Borrow began his famous journey from Chester, celebrated in *Wild Wales*, in the year 1854. After establishing himself for a while at Llangollen he advanced on Snowdonia. His wife and daughter he sent on by coach to Bangor. Himself he walked.

Now Borrow was very much a road walker—in that sense a step back from Pennant. Therefore we do not expect an appreciation of hill scenery as such, or hill climbing. Indeed for a man as arrogant as he normally showed himself there is a pleasing humility in the following observation, made to the Snowdon Ranger of Cwellyn:

I do assure you, friend, to be able to move at a good swinging pace over level ground is something not to be sneezed at. Not that I would for a moment compare walking on the level ground to mountain ranging, pacing along the road to springing up crags like a mountain goat, or assert that even Powell himself, the first of all road walkers, was entitled to so bright a wreath of fame as the Snowdon Ranger.

This may be so, but it was of course a wily compliment and it had its effect. John Morton, the ranger in question, who opened the Snowdon Ranger Inn by Llyn Cwellyn, said of Borrow that he 'never saw a nicer gentleman.'

We expect therefore from Borrow the associations more than the scenery, as he tramps along the road between Capel Curig and Bangor, the first road through the mountains to be properly built (in 1805). After dinner at the Royal Hotel, Capel Curig, 'the inn, or rather the hotel, for it was a very magnificent edifice,' he set off up the Bangor road, noticing Gallt yr Ogof on the left, 'a huge lumpy hill with a precipice towards the road probably three hundred feet high.'[1] He also noticed 'a wretched hovel' which, as all members of the Climbers' Club will be indignant to learn, proved on inquiry of two urchins to be called Helyg. The inhabitants of Helyg were miserably poor and lived by making 'wire-work.'

Borrow went on, but did not so much as notice Tryfan, except in so far as it is 'the second of the hills which stood on the left.' What interested him more was the conversation of a carpenter who walked beside him, about Llyn Ogwen and Nant Ffrancon;

---

[1] See *Climbers' Club Guide to Tryfan*, 1937 ed., p. 92. 'Short rock ridges rise after 200 feet for the last 100 feet to the top.' Borrow had a good eye.

every interesting personality always seemed to meet with Borrow at some time. He covered the thirty-four miles from Cerrig y Druidion in the day and did not feel tired; this being at the age of fifty-one.

But highway-bound as Borrow may seem, there were heights which moved him to a fine poetic frenzy. These were not necessarily the physically beautiful, not those which conjure up Wordsworthian sympathies, but the peaks associated with the bards or Muses of Wales. Thus he climbed Plynlimmon in Central Wales out of respect for its sacred streams, from all of which he felt obliged to drink; and found in Snowdon itself a lodestone of all his literary yearnings. (It is noticeable that, having climbed the mountain once, he refused the Snowdon Ranger's offer to take him up by a different route.)

Snowdon is interesting on various accounts. It is interesting for its picturesque beauty. Perhaps in the whole world there is no region more picturesquely beautiful than Snowdon, a region of mountains, lakes, cararacts, and groves, in which Nature shows herself in her most bland and beautiful forms.

It is interesting from its connection with history: it was to Snowdon that Vortigern retreated from the fury of his own subjects, caused by the favour which he showed to the detested Saxons. It was there that he called to his counsels Merlin, said to have been begotten on a hag by an incubus, but who was in reality the son of a Roman consul by a British woman. It was in Snowdon that he built the castle, which he fondly deemed would prove impregnable, but which his enemies destroyed by flinging wildfire over its walls; and it was in a wind-beaten valley of Snowdon, near the sea, that his dead body decked in green armour had a mound of earth and stones raised over it. . . .

But it is from its connection with romance that Snowdon derives its chief interest. Who when he thinks of Snowdon does not associate it with the heroes of romance, Arthur and his knights? whose fictitious adventures, the splendid dreams of Welsh and Breton minstrels, many of the scenes of which are the valleys and passes of Snowdon, are the origin of romance, before which what is classic has for more than half a century been waning, and is perhaps eventually destined to disappear. Yes, to romance Snowdon is indebted for its interest and consequently for its celebrity; but for romance Snowdon would assuredly not be what it at present is, one of the very celebrated hills of the world, and to the poets of modern Europe almost what Parnassus was to those of old.

To the Welsh, besides being the hill of the Awen or Muse, it has always been the hill of hills, the loftiest of all mountains, the one whose snow is the coldest, to climb to whose peak is the most difficult of all feats, and the one whose fall will be the most astounding catastrophe of the last day.[1]

I find about Borrow's prose a robust flow and beauty of expression which hypnotizes and holds; which lures the mind of any who read about or stride through Wales back to the company of the Titanic old moralizer, who, on a fine May morning, set out from Caernarvon to view Snowdon.

They begin the ascent with guide behind, Borrow arm in arm with his daughter Henrietta, doubtless astonishing other parties by singing in his Suffolk Welsh the Snowdon stanza:

> Easy to say 'Behold Eryri,'
>> But difficult to reach its head.
> Easy for him whose hopes are cheery
>> To bid the wretch be comforted.

And indeed they had an audience. 'We were far from being the only visitors to the hill this day; groups of people, or single individuals, might be seen going up or descending the path as far as the eye could reach.' Higher they went and higher; then a halt, 'having a small lake near us [Llyn du'r Arddu], on our left side, which lay dark and deep under the great wall.' After twenty minutes more, he says, they were on top.

Here ensues a very Borrovian scene. First the oft-quoted view: 'Manifold were the objects which we saw from the brow of Snowdon, but of all the objects which we saw, those which filled us with most delight and admiration, were numerous lakes and lagoons, which, like sheets of ice or polished silver, lay reflecting the rays of the sun in the deep valleys at our feet.'

He then turns to Henrietta, who must have been exceedingly patient—and was doubtless used to it—and delivers a harangue on the name of Y Wyddfa, ending with a poem by Goronwy Owen in Welsh.

Such was the harangue which I uttered on the top of Snowdon; to which Henrietta listened with attention; three or four English, who

---

[1] Everyman edition, pp. 172–4.

stood nigh, with grinning scorn; and a Welsh gentleman with considerable interest.   The latter coming forward shook me by the hand, exclaiming:

'Wyr ti Lydaueg?'

'I am not a Llydauan,' said I.   'I wish I was, or anything but what I am, one of a nation amongst whom any knowledge save what relates to money-making and over-reaching is looked upon as a disgrace.   I am ashamed to say that I am an Englishman.'

I have quoted Borrow at some length, partly because, if he is not in sympathy with the hills as hills (too much to be expected perhaps), yet their moorlands and crags, habitations of the Celtic spirits, have penetrated his heart as their literature had already impressed his intellect.   He is brimful of quotation (which must have been exasperating to the victims) and is himself acquainted with the poets.   Thus it is the people, Welsh above all, who stand out from his pages, squeezed into our vision by the 'delightfully self-complacent, happy, healthy, keen-witted, observant, egotistic, rhinoceros-hided old gentleman.' [1]

For, after all, it was his very provocativeness, bounce, and impossible arrogance that brought the colourful side uppermost in the characters he met.   Fascinated, the reader turns the pages in quest of a new oddity.   So remarkable is the faculty for getting into conversation and drawing the other man out, that it is hard to believe that one and the same Borrow could have met so many interesting persons.   Besides which, here for the first time is an English writer interested *as a writer* in the Welsh cause: prepared to exaggerate, doubtless, prepared to believe all that led to support his cause; and yet winning the reader to that cause too, perhaps more than he won the timid Welsh, whom he bullied with his bastard Cymru and put right on quotations from their own poets.

Borrow's influence was enormous and *Wild Wales* ran to many editions.   It was so enormous in England that it coloured the English view of Welsh history.   As an instance, his version of the Beddgelert legend, now by far the most widely known, was really no more than a popularizing version recently put about by the

[1] A. C. Bradley's description in *Highways and Byways in North Wales.*

hotel proprietors. It is quoted also by Bingley, who gives W. R. Spencer's poem on the subject, that culminating in the stanza:

> 'Hell-hound! my child's by thee devoured,'
> The frantic father cried,
> And to the hilt his vengeful sword
> He plunged in Gelert's side.[1]

But it would hardly have taken hold without Borrow's robust telling of the tale. And now most travellers would quote it to you as the true story. So great is the power of the writer.

10

In more ways than the literary Borrow marks the end of a period. '"I despise railroads," said I, "and those who travel by them."' But most of his countrymen did not, and 'the scum of Manchester and Liverpool' was now taking advantage of them to come swarming up the steeper as well as the easier flanks. Men with no knowledge of the Welsh (that was what particularly riled him) presumed to come and climb the Welsh mountains. Just as the de Saussures and Tyndalls of the Alps had given place to the Leslie Stephens and Mummerys, so in Wales the tradition of the 'ulterior motives' travellers had been transformed into that of the walker for health, the rambler, and every kind of casual visitor. Very soon, from so many diverse persons, there sprang with increasing impetus, and creating a literature of their own, the new race of the climbers.

It has been said already that the first recorded rock climb seems to have been Bingley's and Williams's ascent of the Eastern Terrace of Clogwyn du'r Arddu. But Bingley was on botany bent, and therefore in the old tradition. The activities of the climbers, on 'rocks for their own sake' and also as training for the Alps, lie in another part of this book. However, the taking over of Pen y Gwryd by Harry Owen in 1847 ushers in, besides many mountaineering names, the next four literary figures, themselves

---

[1] Op. cit. p. 246. Beddgelert is in fact a fairly modern village, and the name probably commemorates St Celert.

not in the strict sense mountaineers.   Charles and Henry
Kingsley stayed here, with Tom Hughes, author of *Tom Brown's
Schooldays*, and Tom Taylor, later editor of *Punch*.   From these
emanate many stories, poems, and allusions to the characters they
met; but in Charles Kingsley at any rate there is also a more
serious wish to bring the landscape and life of the district into the
story of his novel, *Two Years Ago* (1857).

It is a period piece and as such had a great success.   Part of the
action takes place at Beddgelert, 'at the easily recognizable Leek
Hotel where ruleth Mrs Lewis, great and wise, over the four
months Babylon of guides, cars, chambermaids, tourists, artists,
reading parties, camp-stools, telescopes, poetry-books, blue
uglies, red petticoats, and parasols of every hue.'   But the
protagonist here, the poet who has changed his commonplace
name to Elsley Vavasour, has no sympathy with this clatter, being
vain and pretentious.   Having ascended Hebog and other heights,
in the confidence that when he gets down everybody will be
saying: 'There goes Mr Vavasour, the distinguished poet.   I
wonder where he has been to-day and what he has been thinking
of,' he is seized with a fit of mad jealousy at his wife's supposed
behaviour towards a certain Major Campbell.   He dashes without
warning up to Pen y Gwryd, and enters 'a low room ceiled with
dark beams, from which hung bacon and fishing-rods, harness
and drying stockings, and all the miscellanea of a fishing inn kept
by a farmer, and beneath it the usual happy, hearty, honest group.'

But he does not pause.   On he goes into the night, up the
recesses of the Glyders, pursued meanwhile by two Oxford men
who believe him (not unreasonably) to have suicidal intentions.
Here Kingsley tries, though not altogether successfully, to tune
his hero's passions romantically to the storm.   Somehow the
storm in this case is a faintly stage storm, a symphonic piece neatly
arranged to suit the mood.

In front of him rose the Glyder Vawr [in fact the Fach], its head
shrouded in soft mist, through which the moonlight gleamed upon the
quarries of that enormous desolation, the dead bones of the eldest born
of time.   So up he goes, upward and upward, ever driven on by the
terrible gadfly, like Io of old he went, stumbling upwards along torrent
beds of slippery slate, writhing himself upward through crannies where

the waterfall plashed cold upon his chest and face, yet could not cool the inward fire; climbing, hand and knee, up cliffs of sharp-edged rock.

Histrionic as this is, it is the first attempt that I know seriously to put a Welsh climbing experience into fiction, or to mingle the emotions of an imaginary protagonist with the scene.   Snowdon obligingly lays the lightning on still thicker for his greater benefit, even as, on a faintly similar occasion, Nature sympathized with the passion of King Lear: 'There it was again!   Lasting but for a moment: but long enough to let him see the whole western heaven transfigured into one sheet of pale blue gauze, and before it Snowdon towering black as ink, with every saw and crest cut out, hard and terrible, against the lightning-glare.   And then the blank of darkness.'

At last the summit plateau, past 'a line of obelisks, like giants crouching side by side' (not a bad description), until he stumbles on to the final crest.   But meanwhile the two Oxford men have found him out, as he lies in a stupor of exhaustion between the boulders.   He is overpowered, and the whole strange party sleeps the remainder of the night out on the mountain top; all except Elsley, who cunningly has kept awake and now creeps away down the hillside, making a dramatic descent into the hollow of Cwm Idwal—by which gully it is interesting to speculate.[1] Thence he continues, demented and without pause, the many miles to Bangor and the London train.   Certainly one of the oddest expeditions ever conceived in Snowdonia.

Less melodramatic and perhaps more sympathetic as scene-painting is Henry Kingsley's chapter on Snowdonia in *Austin Elliott*.   On one occasion Austin himself sits through a summer night of reflection, looking out at but not really seeing 'Snowdon hanging aloft like a purple crystal, and the arch of twilight creeping along it from west to east, through the short summer night, until it begins to flash and blaze into a dawn more glorious than the forgotten sunset.'

Apart from the Kingsleys, there is a description of Ffestiniog and the Cynfal Falls (under different names) in Mrs Gaskell's

[1] In 1888 Sir George Young went over the ground thoroughly and decided it must have been 'the very steep screes, through the gap bordering on Bristly Ridge.'   He was accompanied by his son Geoffrey.

Ruth. But of all the Victorian novels that which most places Snowdon among its characters is undoubtedly *Aylwin* by W. T. Watts-Dunton, in his youth the friend of Borrow, in old age the disastrous protector of Swinburne. With Borrow Watts-Dunton had studied the gipsies, and he edited *Romany Rye*. *Aylwin* (1898) was in part a study of Romany life in its passionate and romantic aspects. In these Snowdon, the appropriate background, had a chance to play a far more integral part than in *Two Years Ago*.

But curiously enough, though in the later chapters it is always there, it is still usually as a decorative back-cloth rather than a stark (absurdly, melodramatically stark) foreground such as Kingsley gave. A young man of wealth, Harry Aylwin, loves Winifred Wynne, the Maid of Snowdon. When Aylwin's father dies, fate decrees that Winifred's father shall violate his tomb, thereby laying himself and his family under a curse. Believing herself accursed, Winifred flees her betrothed, and much of the book is taken up with his efforts to find her. He falls in with the Romany, or gipsies, in particular Sinfi Lovell, a maid of Amazonian proportions with the added power of prophecy. In her company he finds his beloved, temporarily demented, on Snowdon. But after mad converse over a picnic breakfast (near Llyn du'r Arddu?) she suddenly escapes, tripping lightly away across the crags.

With a yell of 'Fy Nhad' and then a yell of 'Father!' she darted round the pool, and then, bounding up the rugged path like a chamois, disappeared behind a corner of jutting rock. . . . I crouched and gazed at Winifred as she glided along towards a vast mountain of vapour that was rolling over the chasm close to her. She stood and looked into the floating mass for a moment, and then passed into it and was lost from view.

The place is too dangerous for Aylwin, but Sinfi follows alone—in vain. Up to the top of Snowdon then they go, and down in their search.

I had not sense then to notice the sunset-glories, the peaks of mountains melting into a sky of rose and light-green, over which a phalanx of fiery clouds was filing; and yet I see it all now as I write, and I hear what I did not seem to hear then, the musical chant of a Welsh guide ahead of us, who was conducting a party of happy tourists to Llanberis.

Photo by G. C. Band

14(*a*). Snow on Y Garn

Photo by J. R. Edwards

14(*b*). Tryfan

So they search, with a thoroughness that reveals a very fair know-ledge of Snowdonian recesses, but in vain. The landscape melts into a gloomy picture of her loss.

After other adventures, during which Aylwin is led to believe that Winifred is dead, he returns to North Wales: 'My love of North Wales, and specially of Snowdon, is certainly very strong. . . . With Wales I actually fell in love the moment I set foot in the country. This is why I am hurrying there now.' Once arrived he shuns the crowds. 'I went to the hotel at Pen y Gwryd, but there tourists and visitors made life more intolerable still to a man in my condition.' He therefore lives alone, now nursing at the back of his mind a growing knowledge that *she* is not really dead. He visits scenes associated with her, and there is a description of the Fairy Glen and Swallow Falls, the latter interesting to compare with Borrow's earlier account. *Aylwin* I find more evocative, but forcing harder after effect to suit the hero's situation.

Bursting like a vast belt of molten silver out of an eerie wilderness of rocks and trees, the stream, as it tumbled down between high walls of cliff to the platform of projecting rocks around the pool at the edge of which I stood, divided into three torrents, which themselves were again divided and scattered by projecting boulders into cascades before they fell into the gulf below. The whole seemed one live cataract of living moonlight that made the eyes ache with beauty.

Borrow had been characteristically more didactic (note for instance the endings of the two descriptions). Going more directly to the point, he gives finally a clearer picture.

. . . two beautiful rolls of white water, dashing into a pool a little way above the promontory; then there is a swirl of water round its corner into a pool below on its right, black as death and seemingly of great depth; then a rush through a very narrow outlet into another pool, from which the water clamours away down the glen. Such is the Rhaiadr y Wennol, or Swallow Fall; called so from the rapidity with which the waters rush and skip along.

Borrow was writing a guide. The impression that Watts-Dunton wished to give was of a place romantically recalling the person. So it is with Snowdon itself. 'I could not leave Snowdon. The mountain's very breath grew sweeter and

L

sweeter of Winnie's lips.'   It is under Snowdon itself that the
Amazon-gipsy is able, with a carefully prepared *coup de théâtre*,
to produce Winnie, who was of course not dead at all.   She is
healed, the curse is resolved, and together they climb Snowdon a
second time.

Ah, that ascent!   I wish I had time and space to describe it.   Up the
same path we went which Sinfi and I had followed on that memorable
morning when my heart was sad as it was buoyant now. . . . Reaching
the top, we sat down in the hut and made our simple luncheon.   On
the descent the beauty of the scene, the touch of the summer breeze,
soft as velvet even when it grew boisterous, the perfume of the Snowdonian flowerage that came up to meet us, seemed to pour in upon me
through the music of Winnie's voice which seemed to be fusing them all.

Here the geography becomes vague.   They drink water near,
apparently, the miners' huts in Cwm Dyli, and yet they are
heading for Llanberis, and also looking at the Menai Bridge.
But no matter; the essential is that they are down, the final bliss
has been given upon Snowdon.

I have lingered over *Aylwin*, because it is one of the very few
novels that I know in which Snowdon plays a *major* role; and it
was, at the time when it appeared, immensely popular, though for
obvious reasons it is seldom read now.   For how little of the real
Snowdon is here, how much is back-cloth affectation and yet
convention, even if the attempt was brave!   Brave it surely was,
making me wish that it had been more often followed up.   Even
to-day a novel on the lines of *How Green was my Valley* remains
to be written about Snowdonia.   And few modern novels are
likely to contain poetry like that of Eos Bradwen, which Watts-
Dunton not inaptly translates:

> Mountain—wild Snowdon for me!
> Sweet silence there for the harp,
> Where loiter the ewes and the lambs
> In the moss and the rushes,
> Where one's song goes sounding up!
> And the rocks re-echo it higher and higher
> In the height where the eagles live.

This is the 'mysterious magic of Y Wyddfa, that magic which
no other mountain in England exercises.'

II

To keep the association with the great *littérateurs* of the nineteenth century I should perhaps mention an ascent of Snowdon in 1870 by the Fitzgerald family, mother, brother, nephew, and niece of the poet.[1] The party itself was amusingly unskilled, and forms as good a contrast as any to the new writers about to appear on the scene. We have hitherto been concerned with writers who for some purpose or other climb. From now onward much of our material will be provided by climbers who, sometimes quite incidentally, write. For the mountaineer as such has come, and come most conspicuously first to the hotel of Pen y Gwryd. As he began to migrate up to the Pass, finding it nearer to the mountains and equally comfortable, with an Owen there too ('So P y P on P y G succeeds, Owen on Owen'), so he developed the literary and cultured approach typical of his new period.

One very brief word must be said about the climbing; brief, since I do not want to trespass on the other chapters. The activities at Pen y Gwryd started as hill walking and developed into roped climbing. We have already seen how the climbers by degrees abandoned other pretexts, botany or angling or geology, to devote themselves self-consciously to plain and simple climbing, along with an enthusiasm for mountain beauty sprung from the embers of Ruskin's, and more especially Wordsworth's, enthusiasm. They found Welsh climbing for its own sake to be a satisfactory sport, but at first they were placed very much on the defensive about the whole business. They wrote defensively; and typical of the time and attitude, as of much of the verse written, but good as only A. D. Godley, the scholar, can be, is this verse apology:

> Cader and Snowdon and Lliwedd and Glyder,
>   What, after all, are formations like these?
> Stratified rocks (if you come to consider)
>   Placed at an angle of x-ty degrees!
> Why should a person provided with reason
>   Batter his bones and endanger his skin,
> Trying in vain to revert for a season
>   Back to the ways of his simian kin?

[1] *Climber's Club Journal,* vol. v, No. 3.

Answer, O climbers of buttress and gully,
　　Writhing in chimneys and wading in snows,
You who have breasted the crags of Cwm Dyli,
　　You who have clung to the Parson his Nose—
Looked from the peak to the limitless distance,
　　Mountain and sea in the rain and the sun,
Tasted the intimate joy of existence,
　　Labour accomplished and victory won:

This be your thought as you turn from the summit,
　　Gripping the rocks as you gingerly go,
There, where the cliff with the drop of a plummet
　　Dips to the scree and the valley below—
Men with a mind on a rational basis
　　Walk on a road (as I'm sure that they should);
Yours are the truly delectable places,
　　Yours is the spice of the Ultimate Good.

If only he had written more often of Wales!

It is noteworthy how eager, forthright, in a sense naïve and yet metaphysical too, the writing near the turn of the century is. Standards which are accepted now by climbers and non-climbers alike were then being formed and justified. Thus in the two hotels particularly circles were formed of sets of friends reassembling year after year, climbing, talking, singing (at P y P), writing on the Welsh hills; finally creating their own tradition of a type of approach unique and important in mountaineering history.

Some of the songs that survived were collected into *Songs of Mountaineers* by John Hirst; the Pen y Pass song at least deserves to be recorded in this book, well known as it still is:

When the wind from Cwm Idwal, Cwm Llydaw, Cwm Glas,
　　Comes welcoming over the scree:
'Come home, mountain friends, to your rest on the Pass,
　　Come back, mountain climber, to me.'

Memorable too is the oft-quoted snatch:

The climber goeth forth to climb on Lliwedd,
And seeketh him a way no man has trod,
But which of the thousand routes he doeth
Is known only to Thomson—and to God!

When the Climbers' Club was formed in 1898 Pen y Pass had not yet been opened (it was opened in 1901, and did not 'supersede' P y G till after 1903). Thus the club was born under the hospitable star of the lower hostelry, in a fandango of dinners, speeches, meets, impromptus, and journal (first edited by E. R. Turner, then by A. W. Andrews). The dinners were formidable affairs, remarkable for speeches as numerous as the courses, of which there were eleven. There would be between nine and thirteen speeches, all reported in a full parliamentary style in the journal, all crammed with wit and quotation and usually bubbling with elaborate personal reference that still reads well. On his supposed defection from the Alpine Club to the newly formed club, Charles Edward Matthews, doyen of Pen y Gwryd, was chaffed characteristically by Douglas Freshfield, with a jibe at the supposed impromptu of his speeches.

> Why is it to the Alpine Club
> Our C. E. M. no longer keeps?
> Why should he found—himself the hub—
> A Climbers' Club for 'chimney sweeps'?

> The answer, Sir, is very clear:
> To give elsewhere those famous speeches
> That flow impromptu year by year
> From your epergne of grapes and peaches.

But it would be a side-track to continue quoting in this field. I will only say that the more vocal and pen-prone of the climbers at and after the turn of the century tended to be the intelligentsia, an aristocracy of letters and the arts with a sprinkling of sciences thrown in. This was natural at that time, since the schoolmasters and dons were usually those with most time to spend and also, as corollary, those most likely to elevate their mountain moods into a sustained way of thought leading to writing. It is instructive, for instance, to notice some of the early contributors to the *Climbers' Club Journal*: A. D. Godley (don) sent verses; W. P. Ker, the medieval scholar, and Mrs Arnold Forster, centre of the Cambridge group which was later to include Rupert Brooke and Mallory, contributed; O. G. Jones (schoolmaster) sent articles which were to form his *Rock Climbing in the English Lake*

District; H. V. Reade (civil servant) contributed, and the Clifton master Dakyns. Besides these, many literary names grouped themselves into the parties invited yearly by Geoffrey Winthrop Young to Pen y Pass: G. M. Trevelyan (historian and don) and George Mallory (schoolmaster); Cecil Slingsby and J. M. A. Thomson (schoolmaster), author of the first *C. C. Guides*; Donald Robertson, a fellow of Trinity, Cambridge; Trevenen and Julian Huxley (Aldous too for a space), Robert Trevelyan the poet, Robert Graves, and many more whose hill writings survive in essay form or whose promise was cut short by the First World War. Geoffrey Winthrop Young himself, from whom much of this information is quarried, I am keeping until later. He too was for a time a schoolmaster.

It is difficult for one who from boyhood has cherished an idolatry of these men of the heroic age to summarize justly their literary contribution. For generalization on Snowdonian history, as on any other historical epochs, is a dangerous pastime. It seems to me, however, that in that first flush of discovery, when the climber came to the glorious awareness that he was 'part with the rock he shoulders,' there was an atmosphere of more conscious idealism in the writing, as well as of greater surface gaiety, than ever since. At its worst it can be this sort of thing: 'However, after your trouble in bringing that pot up that chimney, I'll do my duty at all risks. Here's to you, grand old pinnacle! But bury that pot under a stone, you lazy chap, and pick up the silver paper.' At its best, the spirit speaks in the clear tones of Pope, Winthrop Young, Huxley, C. E. Montague, Conor O'Brien, and a galaxy of others. Here is the self-conscious effort to express directly, often poetically but always forcefully and without relation to common everyday experience, the trials and splendours of the new sport, the new cult.

12

When O. G. Jones was killed in the Alps in 1899, before he could bring out his companion volume to *Rock Climbing in the English Lake District*, the work was taken on by the brothers George and Ashley Abraham, photographers from Keswick.

In 1906 these two brought out *Rock Climbing in North Wales,* a massive volume in style more akin to Pennant than to the modern streamlined guides of Harding, Moulam, Moseley and their peers: discursive, digressive, narrative, laden with personal reminiscence, pen portrait, joke, or poetical tag. It is a guide-book for the library, not for the pocket or even rucksack. Its fine illustrations cost infinite energy and many oaths, since they are all photographs from a bulky plate camera, and the sometimes ponderous humour made the book one of the dear companions of my boyhood, for I think that boys like this sort of thing. It was far nearer and dearer to me than any modern guide could be, belonging as it did to an epoch that is past, an epoch which could straightforwardly enjoy the simpler pleasantries. Take this specimen (in the cave of the Great Gully of Craig yr Ysfa):

Whilst the shower outside gradually subsided, some of us enjoyed a little relaxation in attempting to dispel the damp mist by filling the cave with tobacco smoke. The speleologist was quick to notice the behaviour of these artificial clouds, which seemed to be drawn upwards by a slight current of air. He propounded a theory of a through route somewhere behind the tumbled boulders higher up. . . . If the rest of us had been proof against the wet and cold conditions, I really believe our troglodyte would have excavated himself from the pitch by the through route in about a week's time. He was able to get his head out of the hole, but a bulge of rock on the main wall of the gully stopped further progress . . . so my brother kindly and considerately took hold of his legs and pulled him down the smooth hole to the bed of the gully.

[Op. cit. pp. 91, 92.]

There is a mass of information about climbs in this book, specially to be enjoyed after one has done them. A number of first ascents are described, though it must be said that neither Jones nor the Abrahams had wide experience of Welsh climbing; and there are vignettes of Jones and others. But it was too large to serve the prime purpose of a guide-book, which is to guide climbers up a cliff. There was also at that time a prejudice against the Abrahams, perhaps partly on the score that they were profes-sional exploiters. Nowadays, when not so many mountaineers can lay their hand on their heart and say that the sport has never once turned them an honest penny, and when Himalayan wanderers are forced to sell their pens to Sunday papers in order to win funds, this criticism may seem invalid.   But there was then a feeling against professionals coming to a district and 'exploiting' it for money.   Be that as it may, a series of official volumes was projected by the Climbers' Club.   This meant overcoming the scruples of the more romantic (including J. M. A. Thomson, author with A. W. Andrews of the first volume, on Lliwedd) against guide-books as destroying the charm of mystery.   It was felt, however, sufficiently strongly that much erroneous information was being put about, and that it was the Climbers' Club's duty to tell the true story.

In *The Climbs on Lliwedd* the style is once again of the time, and yet strangely and attractively individual.   It is an impressive period piece, that gives above all a sense of the historic presence of Lliwedd, greatest of Welsh cliffs, and of a mystery about it still that the climbers can no more than probe.   Moreover there is a strong imprint of the quiet, terse personality of Archer Thomson 'poised on one foot on a Lliwedd slab, his statuesque head with its toss of grey curls thrown back, gazing intently upward for the next movement, or crouching solitary on some tiny bracket in space, smoking contemplatively' (G. Winthrop Young).   In style he is much neater than the Abrahams, and at the same time vividly evocative.   A long-standing favourite of my own is the description of the Avalanche Route: 'The most exposed climb in England and Wales.   Exceedingly difficult but delectable in good weather, indefensible in bad. . . .   Excellence of rock.   Exiguity of holds.   Long distances between belays.   A succession of breezy situations.'

Nice too are the lithe descriptive phrases, which one can imagine the authors working out on their 'tiny brackets': 'a fancy foothold of limited utility,' 'a natural cairn built on Nature's liberal scale' and so on.   With the freshness of the exploratory approach the first sensation that wells out of this small masterpiece is

the sheer joy of living,
The leaping from rock up to rock.

This book and *Climbing in the Ogwen District*, which Archer

Thomson brought out a year later, are classics; for however much
each generation may smile at the standards of the one before (and
the description of the Avalanche Route is more fun if you have
done the climb), we remember, first that the art, or craft as some
would call it, of guide-books was in its infancy; and secondly that
this guide reflects brilliantly the great respect in which rock
faces were still held.   The gullies previously favoured were
being slowly deserted.   And the walls and slabs between seemed
very steep and precarious.

13

Among the mountaineers of this pre-First World War period
I must devote a section to Geoffrey Winthrop Young, because his
influence through his writing has been perhaps greater than that
of any other single individual.   This is partly because he had
formed the Pen y Pass tradition of comradeship, scholarship, and
physical activity, so that after 1918 he was able to carry it on into
the between-wars and beyond; partly because he gathered the
wealth of experience gained during those years into the classic
Mountain Craft; and finally, and more aptly to our purpose,
because he was the first, so far as I know, to whom the term
'mountain poet' could justly be applied.   His are the best
known of mountain poems; and there are few mountaineers who
cannot quote 'I have not lost the magic of long days.'   I put
him here because his most active days as a climber were just
before 1914, and his association was with the Pen y Pass
group.

From the Snowdonian point of view, what most concerns us is
the first chapter of *On High Hills*, parts of *Mountains with a
Difference*, and the poems.   *Mountain Craft* is a classic (and a
novelty in its handling of the psychological element in climbing),
many of whose lessons were learnt on Welsh hills; it has a beautifully balanced prose style of its own.   But its scope is too large
for the Welsh compass.   In *On High Hills*, on the other hand,
though the main theatre is the Alps, I have the impression that the

thought behind comes out as clearly in the early as in the great Alpine chapters.   It was on the comparatively *low* hills of Snowdonia that the shape and forms and feel of the mountains, their ridges and rugosities and cavities, their reaction to sun and snow and wind, led him to regard these creatures, mountains, as beings which we do not worship for themselves, but which are 'moving' in their own way 'between the eternal mode and mine.'   And it is interesting to compare this chapter with the return to Wales, one-legged, in *Mountains with a Difference*.   The prose of *On High Hills* seeks already to capture in the sometimes complicated, rhythmical run of its sentences the very complicated rise and fall of the ridges, the essential being of these sculpted shapes.   Here is Snowdon in the first chapter:

On to Snowdon we circled over the falling wave-crest of Lliwedd. . . .   Across the bwlch the summit cone of Y Wyddfa stands against the sunset.   In winter, cairn and sky-crag are plumed with feathers and fern-leaves of ice.   The level rays pour through the ice-fronds from behind, melting all harder outlines into golden haze. And under this burning halo the mass of lower mountain shadows borrows a seeming of transparency and lightness, as if the whole peak were changing into evening cloud, and drifting out towards the sea.

This is primarily a simple picture of a mountain at sunset, but there is also in it, as in the Alpine peaks later, a greater personality which reveals itself when man and mountain come into close sympathetic touch.

The poems move in the same thought.   When the poems from *Wind and Hill*, *Freedom*, and *April and Rain* were collected in 1938 into the *Collected Poems*, the author gave the first book of poetry that I know to be coherently and consciously concerned with man's activity on and relation to the mountain surface; the active, rather than the contemplative state of Wordsworth. This does not mean that *all* the poems are about hills, nor is this a literary review of them.   But it is relevant that the accent is on youth in hills, particularly to my mind the hills of Wales, the poems running with all the speed of many metres through a host of catching word-plays, running and laughing by the water and then, 'in the storm days of our strength,' turning to greater

heights: to the mutability of it all and the comfortingly enduring
quality of the mountains among which we play out our game.

> Look back a thousand years, a thousand more;
> there were then boys afoot by Llydau's shore;
> long-haired, short-kilted, panting through the rocks
> to make a game of shepherding their flocks.
> Other the mountain call, the mountain name:
> but Snowdon looked the same.
>
> Look forward fifty tens, and fifty more:
> there'll still be boys, and still be Llydau's shore. . . .

It was not many who would have gone so far as to wish, with
Geoffrey Young:

> to know of only two
> verities, yourself and the hill you climb.

That feeling comes to most only at certain seasons.   But to
almost all the feeling did come that the corollary to love of mountains was not a passive, Buddhist-type contemplation, but an
intense personal seeking and exploring of every facet; a discipline
of the human body, itself a splendid thing ('these splendid limbs'),
upon a razor-edge of endeavour and hard living.

> In this short span
> between my finger-tips on the smooth edge
> and these tense feet cramped to the crystal ledge
> I hold the life of man.
> Consciously I embrace
> arched from the mountain rock on which I stand
> to the firm limit of my lifted hand,
> the front of time and space:
> > For what is there in all the world for me
> > but what I know and see?
> > And what remains of all I see and know,
> > if I let go?

Reading this poem now I am reminded, perhaps absurdly, of our
later, mid-twentieth-century utterances, less articulate, perhaps
partly because those earlier premises are now accepted, and by a
wider generality of men and women.   I am reminded, for
instance, of the remark attributed to Joe Brown, prodigy of the

Welsh rocks, when asked how he had climbed the fearsome, holdless Cenotaph Corner on Dinas Cromlech.[1] 'Tried hand-jamming right. No good. Tried hand-jamming left. No good. Got up somehow.' I have the impression that nowadays, having accepted the tenets and the situations given us by the pioneers, and climbers being a wider cross-cut of society, we take some pleasure in casting our 'foreheads villainous low,' both about severities and scenery. Like de Maupassant's 'Two Friends,' one of the climbers will say: 'Good, isn't it? A grand climb.' And the other: 'Nice sunset.' Then the two will write, finishing their journal article or postcard home: 'It was a first-class climb, perhaps mild Very Severe. It was six forty-five by the watch when we reached the top.'

Geoffrey Winthrop Young contributed more than anyone I know, through the unforgettable quality of his prose and verse, to this acceptance by climbers of the beauty surrounding them; and of the truth that their own activity in the scene was worth while and therefore need not be talked about.

14

Before passing over the war years I must make mention of a collection of essays which was in part the fruit of Pen y Pass. The Oxford University Mountaineering Club has produced some fine writing, but none better than the *Oxford Mountaineering Essays* (1912), which have been called 'perhaps the most remarkable volume of mountain essays ever produced.' The only one which concerns Wales is 'British Hills' by Hugh Rose Pope, an essay as mature as it is clear and beautifully written. The writer pleads for the (sometimes awesome) intimacy with the hills of the climber, as opposed to the admiration-from-afar of the Ruskinian plain-dweller: 'From across the valley Lliwedd appears as a featureless face, grand only in the sweep of its descent into Cwm Dyli. But to the climber it reveals an infinite variety of rock scenery. There is no flat foreground to detract from the sense of

[1] The central crack in the illustration, Plate 8.

height.   The eye looks straight across a mile of emptiness to the
opposing bastions of Cwm Dyli.'   It is of interest that Pope
sees a cause for lack of due respect to the hills in the 'modern'
ease of access for the city-dweller.   And that was in 1912!

Arnold Lunn, whose energy gathered these essays together,
gave up rock climbing himself after his accident on Cader Idris
in 1922, and went on to give the great impulse to ski-moun-
taineering with which his name is associated.   The accident he
describes in *The Mountains of Youth* (1925), as well as his affection
for Welsh hills (he had been an enthusiastic visitor to the Pass).
He was enjoying their rough rock up to the moment of the fall.
'I have never enjoyed rock climbing more.   I have never enjoyed
rock climbing since.'   And of the hills themselves he says this:

In Wales, more than elsewhere, you are haunted by the ghosts of
kingly ranges which have ceased to be.   You realize the geological
process, not as academic facts, but as the motif of these senescent hills.
The Alps, one feels, are still in their first heady youth, with all youth's
love for bright colours and violent effects.   But Cader and his peers are
the Nestors of the mountains.   They have suffered the incredible
march of time.   They move you with the beauty of old age, calm,
resigned, and aloof.   And their mature wisdom appeals no less surely
to the imagination than the energy of the turbulent Alps.

But the fall of a hundred feet with a loose block on the Cyrfrwy
Arête put an end to rock climbing.   The skiing world gained
what the literature of Snowdonia lost.

15

The First World War came, and removed many of the most
promising.   Those who climbed out of the ashes were slow to
create a new writing, and for some time the old tradition carried
finely on.   One who belongs to it, and who has left a solitary
masterpiece about Wales, is C. E. Montague, with his *A Botanist
in the Hanging Garden Gully*.   This story made me look eagerly
for more, and regret that he did not visit Wales more often.
Montague, who came to Ogwen almost incidentally as the elder

friend of S. W. Herford, makes the assumption that mountains are 'the Right Place,' and treats them with the humour and style of all his other writing.   This short story is well known, yet new at each reading.   The writer, convalescing at Ogwen, joins forces with an ardent botanist possessed of only one sound leg.   Blinded by his passion for climbing, he volunteers to take the botanist up Hanging Garden Gully, the cleft to the right of the Devil's Kitchen, hoping there to find that rarest of plants, *Lloydia*.   After the most hazardous ascent, during which the one-legged botanist is found waltzing out over holdless slab to reach his beloved plant ('My lame Leander gave one whinny of desire.   Then he left all and made for his Hero'), they reach the flat top, which they find to be carpeted with *Lloydia*.   That, briefly, is the story.

But it is in the style, the modesty, the very reserve of the humour that this tale sparkles like a gem.   Here is the crux of the climb: 'This delectable passage was eighty feet high, as I measured it with my experienced eye.   An inexperienced measuring-tape might have put it at fifty.'   'Touché,' the guide-book writer will acknowledge.   Later, when the would-be Darwin leaves the gully to grasp his 'vegetable love' out on the smooth wall, he leaves the rope that connects him with his leader above inextricably entangled behind two chock-stones.   'But life spoils half her best crises.   That wretch never slipped.   He that by this time had no sort of right to his life came back as he went, treading on air, but now with that one bloom of spiderwort in his mouth.'   There remained the rope, jammed behind the chock-stones (since the botanist had taken an outside route):

What to do now?   Climb down and clear the jammed rope?   Leave that lame voluptuary rioting upon a precipice's edge?   Scarcely wise, would it have been?   Puzzled and angry, I cast away shame.   I knew well that as Spartan troops had to come back with their shields or upon them, or else have trouble with their mothers, a climber who leaves his tackle behind in a retreat is likely to be a scorn and a hissing.   Still, I cast away shame.

Montague resembles in many ways A. D. Godley earlier: a master of wit in his own medium; one enthusiastic in his love of rock climbing as of Wales, who, however, through the rigours of a profession, saw less of either than he would have liked.   He belonged in feeling to the earlier rather than the later generation, as did another writer who also, for a different reason, left very little about Wales: George Leigh Mallory. Anybody who has read the first Everest book will agree that Mallory can write finely, and his style was developing. Yet how little there is from him! A few articles in journals, a few essays, and parts of a book. It is very little for a man of thirty-seven, and there is still less that concerns Snowdonia directly. Had the War and Everest not intervened, he and Herford would have carried on the Climbers' Club series of guide-books. And yet this very task presented a difficulty which he felt strongly, that of combining narrative information with good writing. In the case of journals (and guide-books too *pari passu*) he found that 'our periodic literature gives little indication that our performance is concerned less with the spiritual side of us than with the physical. This is, in part, because we require certain practical information of anyone who describes an expedition (or, equally, a rock climb). Our journals, with one exception, do not pretend to be elevated literature, but aim only at providing useful knowledge for the climber.'[1]

And yet, he goes on, what an opportunity there is, once the practical details are over! I sometimes think that, had he lived, Mallory would have used that opportunity; that he would have applauded the work of Saint-Exupéry and brought the skill of climbing, as the Frenchman has flying, into dramatic and significant form. And yet—I am not sure. I am blinded, as all mountaineers must be, by the light that surrounds this legendary figure. I have to remember that some who knew him and admired him still say that he did not write more simply because he was not made that way. His devoted friend A. C. Benson thought very little of his book on Boswell. As a schoolmaster he never reached his full stature, even if Robert Graves (in *Good-bye to All That*) says nothing but good of him. In the years before Everest it seemed that he came together as a person in action and graceful movement rather than words.

All the same, what he wrote of Everest remains so superlatively good that more of like calibre might have been expected on Wales. Especially this force of movement, this life-force unifying into

[1] 'The Mountaineer as Artist,' *Climbers' Club Journal*, 1914.

personality—this might have expressed itself in words.   In the article quoted he thinks that a mountain ascent would be 'a superb theme for an epic poem.'   He takes an ascent of Mont Blanc as symphonic in its possibilities, while Welsh hills would be a humbler melody, their resting-places recurring like chords in the movements.   This thought must have come to him from the parties at Pen y Pass, or the Gorphwysfa, where each year the same faces were to be seen.   'Impressions of things seen return unbidden to the mind, so that we seem to have a whole series of places where we love to spend idle moments, inns, as it were, inviting us by the roadside, and many of them pleasant and comfortable Gorphwysfas so well known to us by now that we make the journey easily enough with a homing instinct.'

What Mallory would have done with his writing had he survived 1924 is matter for guess-work.   He remains a legend.   But the fact of his journal article may serve as an introduction to the writing that followed.   For now increasingly the theme of Snowdonia splits up into specialist departments and favours the medium of articles.   You may be a student of folklore and write about Snowdonian legends; you may be a climber and write guide-books or diagrammatic articles about your latest verticalities; you may be an angler and describe the lake and stream fishing.   You could not now be a Borrow, compassing the whole of Wild Wales in one volume, the work of a professional writer. This means that the best things from the point of view of literature tend to crop up almost casually in the journals of the various clubs and societies.   They are tantalizingly difficult to pick out, to pin-point and say: 'This is permanent, that is not.'   Yet in their sum they make up the literature of Snowdon, as no one book could do.

For a time, in the climbing fraternity, there is a comparative blank.   The world recovers breath, and Wales too.   H. E. L. Porter had in 1921 competently added a supplement to Archer Thomson's Ogwen guide.   In 1926 Herbert Carr brought out a much needed *Climber's Guide to Snowdon and the Beddgelert District*.   Thus the whole of the Snowdonia area was at last covered; and in Porter's supplement, though more definitively in Carr's book, the verbal system of standards (Difficult, Very

15. Nant Gwynant and Moel Hebog

Difficult, etc.) is used, and a standard put beside each climb. There lingers still a pleasing inclination to the picturesque, as in the charming description by Carr of the third pitch of the Overhanging Chimneys in Cwm Silyn.

Here there is a ledge charmingly situated. Peeping hopefully round the base of the Nose, the leader discerns an attractive line of advance on its southern side. A series of steps and an angle crack conduct him to a sloping stance on a vertical wall with the third overhanging chimney out of reach on his right. Hold is provided for the feet, but for the moment there appears to be nothing suitable for the hands. Calling loudly upon the patron saint of the locality, the leader explores the smooth and vertical wall with eager fingers. The saint, responsive to so urgent a request, opens a cunning little cavity in the rock precisely where it is least expected and most desired. The thankful climber is now able to swing out boldly across the wall, and quickly gains the security of the chimney.

While these guides are far less digressive than the Abrahams, there is no sign yet of the laconic terseness of the modern versions. And one other feature must be noticed. This is the only guide in which the walkers are specifically catered for. The first part of the book is devoted, with maps to help, to the walks on these hills: a good reminder, perhaps, that rock climbing should grow out of a love of hill wandering.

I said just now that you could no longer be a Borrow compassing Snowdonia in one volume. But you could get others to help you. In 1925 there appeared the book to whose second edition this present work is rather a supplement than a successor; I mean *The Mountains of Snowdonia*.[1] This book, edited by H. R. C. Carr and G. A. Lister, has sections on the history,

---

[1] For any who have not read the book, the contributors are: Professor J. E. Lloyd on legend and history; E. W. Steeple on nomenclature; G. A. Lister on the coming of the mountaineer and cartography; H. R. C. Carr on the history of Pen y Gwryd and mountaineering; A. Lockwood on angling and the weather, the latter with Professor K. Orton, who also writes on bird life; Edward Greenly on geology; Professor J. B. Farmer on flora; L. J. Roberts on Welsh poetry; E. A. Baker on English literature; G. Winthrop Young on Pen y Pass; C. F. Holland on the Ogwen district; H. Priestley Smith on camping. In the second edition D. D. Pritchard contributes on industry, William Ling Taylor on forestry, H. R. C. Carr on mountain walking, and H. E. Kretschmer on rock climbing between the wars.

M

science, literature, and sport of the district.   The fifteen contributors are men distinguished in different fields, and their total
production is still the standard work on the subject.   The essays
vary, but nearly all are clear in exposition and memorable in
quotation.   Some are outstanding.   They are a quarry for the
seeker after information in the whole range of our subject.   In
the field of climbing this was a summing-up, before the events of
1927 and, in the second edition, after the Second World War.

Finally, as postscript to this period, I quote two poets.   The
direct naïveté of Lionel Johnson's adoration may be excessive for
modern taste; but there is no gainsaying his whole-hearted love.

> Lovely and loved, O passionate land!
> Dear Celtic land, unconquered still!
>   Thy mountain strength prevails:
>   The winds have all their will.
>
> They have no care for meaner things,
> They have no scorn for brooding dreams:
>   A spirit in them sings,
>   A light about them beams.

W. H. Davies, the outstanding Welsh writer in the English
tongue of that time, has disappointingly little.   *A Poet's Pil-
grimage* contains nothing relevant at all.   But when he does look
back from America to Wales, his touch is sure, his rhythm
haunting, his picture of Snowdon, as I like to think it, sharply
evocative:

> What happy mortal sees that mountain now.
> The white cascade that's shining on its brow;
>
> The white cascade that's both a bird and star,
> That has a ten-mile voice and shines as far?
>
> Though I may never leave this land again,
> Yet every spring my mind must cross the main
>
> To hear and see that water-bird and star
> That on the mountain sings, and shines so far.

16

In the year 1927 Fred Pigott and Morley Wood made the first ascent of the East Buttress of the cliff called Clogwyn du'r Arddu on the side of Snowdon.   This climb, together with the ascent next year of the West Buttress, may be taken as the first swallow before the summer of rock climbing that brought forward the names of Kirkus, Edwards, Linnell, Hicks, Bridge, A. B. Hargreaves, Longland, and many others.   Besides the journal articles, there began now to appear as a regular feature Snowdonian chapters in mountain books dealing mainly with other ranges. Of these two favourites may be mentioned which appeared in the twenties, F. S. Smythe's *Climbs and Ski-Runs*, with its dramatic account of the first ascent of Clogwyn du'r Arddu's West Buttress, and Dorothy Pilley's *Climbing Days*, in an early chapter of which is the discovery of the Holly-tree Wall.

At this point I seem to hear the angler or archaeologist or geographer, having contained himself in silent indignation for some time past, burst forth in objection: 'You said that now we come to the specialists.   Very well, but why give pride of place to the mountaineering specialists, the climbing cranks ?   What of the poets or scholars or folklorists of Wales, or even of ourselves ? We spend a lot of time covering paper with pen.'   I must admit the blemish.   But I have already apologized to the Welsh for my Sassenach approach, and referred you to 'Snowdon in Welsh Poetry' by L. J. Roberts; maintaining at the same time that translations do no justice to the original, even if I were competent to give a good selection: and I am not.   As for the anglers and archaeologists and all the other -ists, their work comes mainly, so far as I have read it and with due apologies where necessary, in Mallory's category of 'practical information'; very useful, but not primarily literature.   It is perhaps paradoxical that the spark should flash most brightly in the climbers, but so it seems to be. I do not mean in their writings *as* climbers; not in this sort of thing: 'We climbed a V-shaped groove, forty feet.   This brought us to a heathery ledge.   The narrow overhanging crack rising from the right-hand end of the ledge needed one piton for security.'   I mean that mountain activity has continued to attract men of a certain bent; men who, when they are not wrestling up the next overhang or exploring the next hand-jam crack, have a detachment of mind, a singleness of outlook which comes at times near to the poetic. If Shelley had lived a little later, he might have been a bad mountaineer rather than a bad mariner.

As the thirties rolled on, many more were coming to the hills. The literature of the journals was becoming more and more scattered, mixed with more and more sheer bad writing. The climbers that I have mentioned left descriptions of their climbs, some of which must be called good, for the terseness and nimbleness of writing and the vigour of the feats described. I must be content with two examples. In the sparing directness of Colin Kirkus there was a sympathetic force and shy pride corresponding to his climbing and his person. The descriptions of his classic ascents are models of clarity and simplicity. Very little had to be changed in his account of his route on the Cwm Silyn Slab when it came to writing a new guide to that area. And the same with his *Glyder Fach*, brought out in 1937. It is a workmanlike guide, the second of the new series and nearer to the Lakeland than the Edwards style. But there is colour and character about many of the descriptions which make it highly readable in its own way.

Colin Kirkus was by profession a black-coated worker in Liverpool. His excursions to the hills, on foot or by bicycle if he could not afford the train, were life itself to him. In this he is the prototype of many since. In conscious thought his was the practical approach of the route-finder and technician; in fundamental belief he was a poet

> filled with such desire
> As prisoned birds must have in freedom,
> Winging wildly across the white
> Orchards and dark green fields; on; on; and out of sight

—on to the hills. Together with the wild desire to escape from the humdrum of the city he had an equal anxiety not to be sloppy or lose form over this escape, but to look at and think of it as a practical proposition. Thus there is no consciously fine writing in him, and nothing that the ordinary man—or boy—faced with the same anxiety (as we all are) cannot understand. That is why *Let's go Climbing*, his book written primarily for boys, achieves so excellently its purpose, of introducing beginners in a friendly way. The line of personal and sympathetically amicable approach succeeds; he takes the aspiring boy at once into his confidence. It is a game, in which they are in league. 'Before I was twelve years of age I was allowed to wander over the mountains on my own. This shows the value of training one's parents from the very earliest age. I found that, properly managed, they gave very little trouble.' To us here it is of chief interest that all the early and many of the later and great climbs described are Snowdonian. But most of the climbing is simpler than these; for this is a boy's book, and the contents might be any boy's ambition.

The climber in Menlove Edwards, as in Colin Kirkus, cannot be unravelled from the writer. There is a total approach which embraces both. Menlove Edwards, practising psychologist in the thirties, made of his spare time, in writing as in climbing, a medium expressive of his opposition to matter, as to fear. He neither climbed nor wrote easily. On the rock there was a struggle between immensely strong limbs and spirit on the one side; on the other steepness, looseness, vegetation, all the tugging gravity that Welsh rock can offer. As a climber Menlove is described already. When he was writing, the medium of paper and ink represented something equally to be wrestled with; and the poetry in him wrestled with the psychology which he practised too. His output is very small, and every sentence bears the stamp of effort put into it. Also, he characteristically and generously gave up much of the not too plentiful wrestling-time to work for the Climbers' Club on the new series of guides. *Cwm Idwal* (1936), *Tryfan* (1937), and *Lliwedd* (1939) are his creation.

To begin then with the guide-books. These, on two of which I had the privilege of collaborating as junior partner, were the first since Carr, in the twenties, finished the work of Archer Thomson. Meanwhile there had appeared the series of Fell and Rock guides to the Lake District. These were very emphatically pitch by pitch accounts; Menlove used to describe them as a spotlight moving up a cliff, not any cliff in particular, for the spotlight would give you no idea whether you were on Twll Du or Kern Knotts.   It is just a cliff, and if you get the right start you should be able to follow the hand-and-foot instructions.   If you don't you are lost.   I have said that Colin Kirkus's guide is nearer to the Lakeland model (though that statement over-simplifies), and is perhaps the most popular in style of the Welsh guides. Edwards's purpose was to give the type of climbing involved, the sort of lines, groove or chimney or slab, to go for when in doubt.   Here then is the Holly-tree Wall above Idwal, to my mind unrivalled as an exposition of cliff structure:

The Wall has a frontage of about 200 feet and is roughly 150 feet high.   The angle of the face keeps very high without showing many overhangs, or even true verticals of any extent.   The tendency of the rock masses to run up in smooth rectangular blocks with vertical cracks adds considerably to the apparent inclination.   When on the cliff, this arrangement gives perhaps less feeling of exposure than would a curved or slanting line.   There are few ledges, but those few are good and solid.   The whole structure tends to be squared off into blocks divided by cracks, jutting out slightly to form the feature of the face.

The rock itself is of the type seen in the slabs below, rough rock forming a smooth face with cracks at some distance from each other. It is along these cracks that the weathering has given its best holds.

The main structure is uniform and makes a typical climbing geography.   The holds are of all types.   Incuts, large and small, square holds, sloping holds and pockets, are all well represented.   The cracks are mostly narrow, but vary greatly in their facilities. . . .

The careful account thus leads the visitor, wondering what he can manage, to the conclusion that 'often the climbing is of a muscular type, thanks to the preponderance of a few good holds. A spasmodic touch necessarily goes with all this, and this feature, the steepness of the whole and the delicacy of position, are the common factors of the Wall.'   When to this are added obvious landmarks on the face, the climber has received, besides his pleasure in reading, a knowledge of what sort of country he is about to pass through.

Controversy about the writing of guide-books has raged and perhaps always will rage inconclusively.   In an ideal world they would be a pity, for each would go out to discover the Delectable

Mountains for himself. But in the sad real world there is a demand for them which would be content with the worse if the better were not to hand. Men and climbers' clubs are vain enough to think that they can produce the better; in Edwards and Kirkus they found it. Edwards's books are masterpieces, but inimitable. In lesser hands, how could phrases such as 'just mild Very Severe, in technique only' survive? No other personality could successfully tread the same path.

In his other writing the story is the same; only here it is the climber's own state of mind that is being explored. Nearly all of what he wrote is in journals, or unpublished in manuscript. In all these is intense effort (a labour impressive to watch) to reach below the surface of a man climbing—or rowing the Minch, or canoeing to the Isle of Man—into the springs behind him. The verse is not easy and the metre uneven at times, in a way however nowise marring the total effect.

> You rock, you heaviness a man can clasp,
> You sturdy buttress block for hold,
> You, frozen roughly to the touch,
> Yet what can you?
>
> Can you stand over me, suffused,
> And treading lightly for my love?
> Or when I yearn for you, can you
> Recover?   Or could you seem best?
>
> Oh, you can be for praises for my grasp;
> If thin's the heart, you can be cold,
> Or if resolved, you too can such.
> Canst add to me?
>
> Look how the wind is treading, fleet
> Along the lake.   It ripples down
> The mountain-waters of the heart,
> Crossing, recrossing on the breast.

But I may not extract and do justice. Using the mountain experience as starting point, the writer goes deeply down and far beyond for motive.

> He was a Great Climber. He said:
> 'Climb, but I don't know why.'

And only in dream, as to many things, is that answer given. It is sad that the poems are not collected and available to a wider judgment.

For this revelation of states of mind, in the case of climbers above all, prose serves more immediately. If his biggest imaginative achievement is 'Scenery for a Murder' in the *Climbers' Club Journal*, 1939, considered by many to be among the best things ever written for any journal, I think that 'A Great Effort (*Climbers' Club Journal*, 1941) is at once the most amusing and penetrating satire on climbing states of mind that I know. On a cliff in North Wales, not far from the ground, the climber climbs and, as not uncommonly happens, finds himself stuck.

After twenty minutes I had advanced about fifteen feet and was trembling slightly, not too sure of my position. The rock now before my face was ordinary rock, surfaced at an angle of sixty to seventy degrees, fairly smooth. Heaven was above, the earth a few yards beneath, and I remember nothing of either. As for myself, the fore part of my right foot was planted well on a square ledge, the heel overhung into the air and demanded a constant muscular effort at the calf; my left foot was three feet higher and one and a half feet to the side, put against a small sloped piece of grooving. In appearance therefore, had anyone been passing, I was about to step up. In practice I had been trying to do this for ten minutes but had not yet succeeded. It seemed simple, the need was clear, holds were there, but they were small and I am not a man in any way to make a move until satisfied that it is safe, so that to remain in this statuesque and silly position was my only choice for the time being. Every minute or two, when my right leg began to tremble, I pulled the left leg down from its unserviceable height, bent myself this way and that a little to relieve the strain, then put the leg back again, using the action also as a gesture of purpose.

The quotation at length is not irrelevant; for this sensation—and position—on Welsh cliffs are the meat and drink of the average climber. And while Menlove Edwards was in no sense average, either as climber or writer, he knew exactly the struggles that haunt every pursuer after steepness. He used to say that he sometimes quite failed to get up Hope, and it was the truth, for his climbing more than that of most was a thing of mood. In what follows he plumbs another thought common to all who are honest enough to admit it.

Then I thought perhaps if I eat my sandwiches that will improve me, but no, no for shame, it is not yet half past eleven how can I eat them now, yet there can be no harm in it, give yourself a change I said eat them all and that will be a load off your mind, then you will not have the temptation to eat again till you get home. So standing still on my footholds and feeling firmer than I had done for some time, I got the tin of sardines out of my pocket, twisted the lid off in the usual way but carefully because of the position, and ate the fish one by one with my mouth. . . . Now how will it go I thought, every excuse is exhausted. And I tried again. No, it is no good, I said, it is no good.

Snowdonian writers might have served literature even more finely if they had followed yet further the line of these Joycean musings. A day in the climbers' life on the scale of *Ulysses*, honestly told, might reveal heights and depths undreamed of behind the motives alleged by climbers. No novel that I know has so far gone deeply in this direction. It would perhaps be a sordid, but certainly a revealing business.

> The climbers, they,
> They and their hills.
> They come noisily. . . .

Menlove Edwards could have done it, since he had the perception and also the power to his writing. Nully Kretschmer might have done it too, I think, so far as can be judged from the scattered bits and pieces left at his sad death. His mind worked a little in that way, with something of Ibsen thrown in as an afterthought.

In one other form, meanwhile, Snowdonia was continuing to appear. As Welsh (and all British) climbing played a great part in the formation of most mountaineers, so these hills featured and still feature in books recounting personal adventure among many ranges. I have mentioned two such in the twenties. R. L. G. Irving's *Romance of Mountaineering* helped to bring on many more, particularly after the Second World War. Scott Russell's *Mountain Prospect*, Janet Adam Smith's *Mountain Holidays*, Douglas Busk's *The Delectable Mountains* all feature Snowdon as a stepping-stone, early or later, in the author's progress. For

myself, these mountains were the first that I trod and remain my
first love.   When I was infected by the current epidemic of
writing a book containing the word 'mountain,' I tried to give an
account of that devotion in *Mountains and Men*.

In none of these books is Snowdonia the leading lady; she is an
important character, however, and the books are of importance,
linking as they do exploits at home with those in wider fields.
Wales is part of the total experience.

17

The majority of our good writing has been prose.   But what of
poetry meanwhile?   She, poor thing, continues to live and move
and have her being in a welter of verse not all worthy of the
Awen inspiring eisteddfods.   Many journals admit poems, some
of them in small corners rather like the less respectable artist
brothers of business men.   Sometimes they appear interspersed
in a book, as in Showell Styles's *Climber in Wales*.   Or they may
be fragments extracted from a whole like the writing of Michael
Roberts, poet and mountaineer, for whom Wales was a home too.
A younger poet who lost his heart to hills is William Bell.   Bell's
main concern, of course, was with the Highlands, and Scotsmen
may resent the attempt to usurp him; but he was after all a
North Irishman.   As a member of the Oxford University Mountaineering Club he visited Wales, and in 1944 had a bad fall on
Tryfan.   In 1948 a man of strange promise died when with three
Oxford companions he fell to his death on the Matterhorn.

Most of Bell's best poems, published posthumously in *Mountains beneath the Horizon*, contain mountains; many are cast as
elegies or sonnets of classical mode.   He comes into our picture
of Snowdon for several reasons, and especially because that mountain more than almost any is a scene of release as well as of intense
effort for many thousands every summer and every winter.   Now
Bell expresses in poetry of great beauty this struggle of modern
man, away from an increasingly mechanical age towards an outlet
in poetry and the hills, in effort and love.   But there is the

concomitant thought that this outlet and release are themselves
not easy, since the elements to which we escape are still 'other.'

> Although you move among them as a friend
> these mountains cannot take you for a brother.

For after the Tryfan accident the idea of falling, of being pushed
off as it were, occupied him.   Men and these natural objects, these
mountains which they climb and on which they prove themselves,
are 'different,' and their differentness is another aspect of the
struggle as well as the connection between them. The 'two veri-
ties' here take on a sense of opposition, of antagonism even, while
at the same time only through his activity here and away from the
normally clogging environment can man reach spiritual satisfaction.

There are no poems that can be laid directly at the door of Snowdon, but many which might be.   I think of Snowdon when I read:

> for he remembers that he must at length
> be conquered by a more drawn out disease,
> remembers how his ancient height and strength
> have fallen about his feet in trickling screes.

That is the impression that many have had of Snowdon, and
longed to put into words (see Arnold Lunn, page 159): ancestor
of mountains that once towered and now slowly, slowly is being
levelled to the plains.   In physical fact the mountain was the
Tödi; in imagination it was Snowdon too.

At the end of the book is a poem that is both a memory and
perhaps a presentiment, the poem 'On a dying boy.'   William
Bell was himself at last broken on the rocks, as he had been all but
broken in 1944.   His spirit too left the narrowing world, as other
rare spirits have done in youth; left it for another, where we
cannot help feeling, against all reason, that Snowdon and Siniol-
chu, Tryfan and Trisul, Moelwyn and Matterhorn are equal.

> Oh leave his body broken on the rocks
> where fainting sense may drown beneath the sound
> of the complaining surf.   His spirit mocks
> our ignorant attempts to hem it round:
> as eagerly as body sought the ground
> into its native ocean must it flow.
> Oh let his body lie where it was found,
> there's nothing we can do to help him now.

Bell's was not an escape into hills, but a fusion of hills with work which he considered the most important for him, poetry. That is the case with many in these post-war days, though the work may not be poetry, but haberdashery or engineering. The mountains are so real to them that either the work must fit or its reality go. Thus the two ideas of writing and climbing tend more and more to converge; the 'literature' ceases to be on the periphery of the circle, so to speak. It comes in, to lose its character as literature maybe, but to take its place in the cycle of social change.

18

I have said earlier that there is still a fair field of opportunity for the novelist in the Welsh setting. Already in the thirties the novels of Joanna Cannan and Ethel Mannin had shown that mountaineers and mountain dwellers could be subjects for study in fiction. But the line was not followed up. The first good modern Snowdonian novel that I know is *Mountain Rescue* by Douglas Hewitt (1951). True, it is Snowdonian only in the widest sense, since no real places are mentioned and the crag of Craig Du is a mysterious synthetic creation. But there is a breath of reality about every touch of the descriptions given.

A distinguished physician, Martin Russell, is staying in North Wales. He is one of those who are lonely by nature, but he has come to terms with his loneliness through mountaineering, since mountains too are lonely beings indifferent to right and wrong, to love and temptation. Into this self-sufficiency there obtrudes a prisoner of war, Kurt, who has escaped from a camp near by. Out of dislike for the soldiers pursuing him, Russell shelters Kurt in an excellent hiding-place in the hills. The book is a study of his increasingly emotional relations with Kurt and others after that.

Of course this is not a true mountaineering novel, and in some ways it is the better for that. But it is most certainly a *mountain* novel, and the inevitable end takes place in one of the best descriptions of a fall and of a man dying from that fall that I know.

As he stepped down, facing inwards, from the ledge to a lower foothold, before swinging back into the groove of snow, he glanced up at Kurt, who was beginning to move again. In the instant that he took his attention from his own movements, one foot slipped from the rock and, with a jerk, the other. His weight came on his arm. He hung for a moment, scrabbling with his other hand for a hold, while the mushy snow under his fingers hardened with the pressure into a boss of ice, before his hand slid off. His feet hit the rib three feet lower and as he swayed backwards, the rib receding from his clutching hands, he knew that he was going outwards down the face of the buttress.

The black rock blotted out Kurt's face, the skyline circled and plunged away, the glowing sky filled his eyes.

And so, after a scene with Kurt which is full of love, he dies peacefully the death which is the only solution to the emotional tangle in which he has wound himself: 'He lay back, listening to the sound of streams that he had heard before at night from the cave. The balance of sound was different from here. . . . Going, he closed his eyes and listened in the darkness to the steady throbbing of the streams, draining ceaselessly out to the valley from all the hillsides that surrounded him.' The end, like the emotional climax, is achieved with a neat economy of words. In fact the prose throughout is tense yet sparing, a fit robe to a remarkable study.

In 1951 there appeared another book much more directly a climbing novel, as also more of a novel about Snowdonia. In *One Green Bottle* Elizabeth Coxhead may have started a new direction in mountain writing, since her book is unlike any that have before treated of Snowdonia. It is the Odyssey of Cathy Canning, a girl from the meaner streets of Birkenhead. At the beginning the chance that her supposed boy-friend is put away in Borstal leads her to accept the invitation of Leonard Head (whose motives are none of the purest) to visit North Wales for a weekend. Abandoned by her knight at the foot of the Idwal Slabs, while he goes off with a better party, she is tempted to try the easy way; and inevitably gets stuck. Then, rescued by two youth hostellers, Harry and Stan, she is introduced abruptly to a new way of life, to the life of the thousands who pour each week-end, by motor-cycle or hitch-hike, into Snowdonia. Week after week, as she herself starts coming to the youth hostel, she realizes more poignantly the squalor of her own home and background, and the drab future of the boy to whom she was not indeed engaged, but towards whom an artful mother and her own growing loyalty are urging her. By degrees she has mastered the technique of rock climbing, and the climax of the book from that angle comes when she does her first lead on Clogwyn du'r Arddu. Then, on the crest of this achievement and of a real love for a young school-teacher, she finds that the new moral fibre, which climbing and Christopher have given her, demands that she should do the fine thing, go back and greet the worthless Birken-head boy when he returns to freedom. The story ends with her farewell to the sympathetic warden of the hostel, Dorothy Elliott, and the lonely figure tramping off bravely down the Ogwen road. It is a moving end, though unsatisfactory artistically, since the reader cannot help feeling that the sacrifice is cruelly unnecessary.

There are really two aspects of this book, the first more important to the novel as such, the second to the general climate of Snowdonian (or any mountain) writing. The first is the study of the development of a personality, and this is given with a really remarkable depth of insight. Elizabeth Coxhead spares nothing to lay on thick Cathy's initial amorality. From the moment when she consents to sleep with Leonard Head, whom she dis-likes and despises, in order to be given a pair of climbing boots, we know what we are in for. And this side of Cathy's character and experience is stressed, perhaps even too thoroughly and continuously. Certainly I have never observed at youth hostels or on the hills some of the happenings that seem to be common-place here; nor a university lecturer (Oxford, be it said) so despicable as Michael Derwent, the unfaithful fiancé of Dorothy and the one really nasty character in the book. But the important theme is the slow winning of a personality through the variety of this experience, which is given in abundance for that purpose. Sometimes she stumbles and falls; sometimes she is crude and surly-tongued; sometimes, in her own words, 'a tart.' Always she is sympathetic, until we come to love her as Christopher loved, when it seemed to him 'that the face she turned to the rock must be tender and charming.' That is why I cannot be convinced by the ending, though it is made inevitable so far as means allow. It offends to think that she should go back, *without any plan for ameliorating it,* to the pit from which she has hoisted herself. Perhaps she will bring Bill climbing? But it seems unlikely.

In the climbing narrative there is a sincerity and a knowledge of the subject that please. It may be true that the author has not done climbs herself as hard as those of the principal characters (the impossible Johnny Hollinger for instance), but she must have done a great many,[1] and there is a ring of the genuine article about every description of a climb. Very true too is the feeling, which at last penetrates even the material-minded Birkenhead consciousness, that there are hills behind these rocks. At first Cathy, like most of the youth hostellers, despises 'walking.' It is by degrees that a realization comes to her that there is a mountain presence behind, which has no regard for the type of activity you indulge in upon the slopes. On a dramatic rescue at the foot of the Central Arête, Glyder Fawr, she finds herself alone with the badly injured Doreen, who has fallen.

If you keep quiet you can hear the mountains. Slowly to Cathy, as she lay there in the darkness, the mountain became real. First it had been scenery; then a playground, stood up in the air for her amusement, neatly divided into pitches, crowned with a cairn at the top. And now at last it had its own life, independent of her pleasure, terrible, remote; its own laws, which her friends had been trying all these weeks to teach her, and to which she had carelessly, impatiently conformed. At any moment she might have forgotten them, and it only needed a moment, a second of forgetfulness for the mountain to take its revenge. A jaunty figure in a blue jacket swung up out of sight round a corner, and a few hours later was lying like a crumbled eggshell on the mountain's breast.

She was showing me, thought Cathy. And if it hadn't been for Stan, I was going to show her.

That is the blossoming of character, that realization of a truth.

---

[1] The Vertical Vice seems to have got on to the wrong Glyder. But this could be artistic licence.

The second point that I would make about this novel is that it is much more broadly based than the earlier fiction. It has been made clear elsewhere that climbing nowadays is very far from being confined to the strata which could afford it, the schoolmasters, dons, clergymen, and civil servants who found a common joy in hills and most of whom knew one another. Elsley Vavasour, Austin Elliott, Harry Aylwin are the creations of a group whose intellectual interests bound them together. These protagonists talked the same language and would have mixed socially. But Cathy Canning is the first literary representative that I know of the myriads hitherto voiceless, of the factory hands, technicians, shopwalkers, office girls, unemployed, builders' assistants, army privates, and the rest, who swarm out every week to mountain holidays which they contrive to have at next to no cost. And there is an amusing hint here of the original, not unnatural antagonism between these newcomers and the recognized climbing clubs, which liked their hills to themselves. The Everest climber, Sharland, is heard to remark to his companion, when the hostellers are shouting about on the top of Tryfan: 'My fault, old man, for dragging you up Tryfan on a Sunday afternoon.' This supercilious tone is preserved until the accident to Doreen Lord brings the Everester to the youth hostel and the barriers are broken. In the world of reality they have been broken too, so far as they ever existed: partly because many of the newcomers are climbing superlatively well, and no one can be supercilious with somebody he admires; in part more simply, because the hills have always been a common ground for all who could get to them, and activity among them is, ultimately, a unifying thing. It is for this reason that Cathy Canning, eloquent for the multitudes hitherto silent, appeals vividly to a sense of artistic rightness; and that this is a very important book.

What else can fiction offer? The writers of thrillers have not omitted Snowdon from their pages. In *A Throne of Bayonets* (1952) Kevin Fitzgerald sets one of the final scenes in the bar of Pen y Gwryd (Pen y Gwynant), where a dramatic revolver battle takes place. For convenience the occupants are streamlined to three, an unlikely number in the summer months. Mr Briggs (Higgs) is heavily involved, and the battle followed by a further

breathless duel over the cliffs of Lliwedd. Here again, the possibility of being able to enjoy a quiet pitched battle on Lliwedd
between May and September is remote, pleasing as it is to imagine
the villains' death cries resounding from the familiar Horned
Crag. A vivid and violent story. And now Mr Higgs reappears, in an excellent chapter of *It's Different in July* (1955). An
agreeable character, in caricature.

'No woman, or man either, who has climbed Brant is a criminal, let
alone head of a criminal organization.'
'Supposing she didn't climb Brant?' Feston said.
'Then she wouldn't have said she had. No climber in all the history
of climbing has ever said he'd got up anything when he hadn't.'
'Supposing she isn't a climber?'
'That's no good. She talked about the hard move on the first pitch
and the vee chimney on the crux.'
'So could I, if I wished, Mr Higgs. I too have read Mr Harding's
Guide to the Climbs in Llanberis Pass.'
Mr Higgs paled and gulped at his beer. 'You'll have me smoking
next,' he said. . . .

For specifically detective fiction, there is Showell Styles with
Death on Milestone Buttress, a good puzzling story on the classic
crag. The murder situation is genuine, and evolves with proba-
bility out of a genuine climbing situation. *Death under Snowdon*
is not properly concerned with the mountain, despite an opening
chapter on the Horseshoe and a later one about a magnesium-
mine. Nor, really, are the three *romans de cap et d'épée,* though
The Rising of the Lark has Beddgelert as a part of its scenery, and
Sir Devil the Ogwen Valley. The most serious claimant is
Land from the Sea (1952), a lively reconstruction of the scene at
the beginning of the last century, when the Traeth embankment
was being built and the enthusiasts expected Tremadoc to rival
Liverpool. The stormy Madocks and the poet Shelley move
among a network of nationalists, soldiers, chieftains, and poli-
ticians, most of whom have some historical possibility.

But when all is said, it must be admitted by the most generous
that the fiction haul is not large, even if I allow that some English
fish have slipped through my net along with all the Welsh ones.
Yet it is on the road of fiction, and poetry too, that the future may

N

lie.　Certainly there are monumental works of fact still to come, some exhaustive of a particular facet, some having only a small niche for this little land in the great edifice.　Every aspect will be explored, if it has not been explored already, every stone charted and every seasonal mood explained.　For the mountaineer pure and simple there may remain one major summing-up in perspective to be written; but now that White Slab has been climbed, and Dinas Cromlech and the East Buttress of Clogwyn du'r Arddu girdle-traversed, there can surely be no more, unless it concern artificial aids for overhangs.　The pioneer of bigger routes must turn to Scotland and beyond.

Yet there will always remain novels to be written.　First, about the people of Snowdonia and their occupations.　Of this kind *How Green was my Valley* may serve as example.　The shepherds and farmers, bards and miners will here be found; but the quarrymen of Blaenau Ffestiniog and Nant Peris, and the miners who tramped, every week-end and back Sunday night, over the Glyders' shoulder from Cwm Dyli to Bethesda—all these are also worthy themes for a story.　Of the shepherds we know something already from books such as Thomas Firbank's *I Bought a Mountain* (1940), the autobiography of an Englishman who set up as sheep farmer on the rough Glyders.　It is an absorbing account: the intricacies of purchase, the tough plying of a profession over ground where most think only of pleasure, the story of shearing and sales, of snowfall and rounding up, the quizzical shepherd's-eye view of the climber, who goes scampering past the farm, not having time to look round, towards his chosen cliffs.　Firbank admires, is amused, and sometimes a little horrified.　He has an eye for a type, which would go well in fiction.　The countryman of Snowdonia awaits his Hardy, or perhaps Emily Brontë, in winter, when the moors are bare.

The second line of new country concerns, of course, the climbers and tourists themselves.　There may be two sorts of writing, and they may be mixed in differing proportions.　First the social study, of the mix-up of what used to be called 'classes' on this common ground.　The study might be carried on, where *One Green Bottle* left off, with the reaction of those who climb together, when they suddenly face familiarity with each other's background.   The hills are, in this sense, both a link between different types and a delusion; because it is possible to climb with, and be very close to, a companion for many years, and never know anything at all about him away from the magic thread of the rope. The very multiplication of clubs in these days is a token of a greater diversity of approach, which might, somehow, be pictured in vignette.

Secondly in the second type there is the 'psychological' novel. Not necessarily the serious stuff, and any aspirant should have read *The Ascent of Rum Doodle*, not to mention Stephen Potter. But the caricature, as the Rum Doodlists will allow, need not obliterate the reality.   The passion to climb goes deep; and in, for instance, a really close study of a climber's inside workings, with every shade of his feeling towards Snowdon, the rocks, and his companions, the writer will reach something far wider than our present scope.   Take Donald Robertson's dictum, which is true still to-day, that a truly honest account of a climbing day remains to be written.   And start from there, as Menlove Edwards started.

The social and the psychological are not, of course, in any way specifically Snowdonian.   The same changes are going on, the same self-explorations, in the Lake District and in Scotland. But the truly Snowdonian writer will add to whatever he writes a flavour of homage to this particular district which is *Welsh*, with all that means, and which catches at English hearts too.   Here, I think, we Sassenach writers are, in the last resort, at a disadvantage.   We may, as I have, come to these hills in early childhood and have been coming ever since.   We may write from our heart a tribute to the known and loved shapes that greet us each time (if mist allows!) that we top the rising road beyond Cerrig y Druidion.   We may catch in words the activities of climbers and farmers, bards and shepherds, geologists and gipsies, as they move among them.   But we cannot place ourselves under their skin. We cannot feel with immediacy, even as we speak the words, that Bwlch y Saethau is that Pass of the Arrows where King Arthur fought his last battle; Moel yr Hydd the hill of the deer and Pen yr Oleuwen the hill of the white light.   To express ourselves we must turn to a dictionary of ideas.   And I think that in our

English writing there will always be a longing for what we can see and love, but never truly possess; for what only the Welshman,[1] living in his own valleys, savouring their mist and legend, can ever fully enjoy.　Perhaps he is even now building his monument in their tribute.　Perhaps, wisely, he leaves us to clamber our short season over the cliffs and moors into forgetfulness, or to go on trying to put into words what we can never say, though the effort to say it will hold us entranced even to the end.

[1] In this connection, note the two recent books of poetry given in the bibliography.　Professor T. H. Parry-Williams, to whom I am indebted for these, says that there is all in all disappointingly little at the moment.　But the poem *Cwm Dyli* is Snowdonian, and William Jones has a sonnet 'Eryri' beginning:

> Mae balchder yn yr hen fynyddoedd hyn,
> Ac yn eu trem mae pendefigaidd her.

> (There is pride in these old mountains,
> And in their aspect there is a noble challenge.)

Two short lyrics, 'Y Cnicht' and 'Y Moelwyn Bach a'r Moelwyn Mawr,' should also be mentioned.

Let us only hope that the Welsh writers have not been driven by the crude Saxon from their own hills.　Of prose there is very little indeed; but a Welshman of the calibre of Charles Evans, great in action besides, has a chance here.

APPENDIX

A SHORT BIBLIOGRAPHY

The Travellers

GIRALDUS CAMBRENSIS: *Itinerary through Wales*, 1188.

JOHN LELAND: *The Itinerary in Wales*, 1536–9.

WILLIAM CAMDEN: *Britannia*, 1586.

JOHN SPEED: various publications, and maps, 1610.

MICHAEL DRAYTON: *Poly-Olbion*, 1612.

THOMAS JOHNSON: *The Itinerary of a Botanist*, 1639.

JOHN TAYLOR (The Water Poet): *A Short Relation of a Journey through Wales*, 1652.

EDWARD LLWYD: Translation with additions of Camden's *Britannia*, 1695.

LORD GEORGE LYTTLETON: *Account of a Journey into Wales*, published as appendix to editions of Wyndham and Bingley, 1756.

JOSEPH CRADOCK: *Letters from Snowdon*, 1770; *An Account of Some of the most Romantic Parts of North Wales*, 1777.

THOMAS PENNANT: *Journey to Snowdon* (from *Tour in Wales*), 1781.

REV. W. BINGLEY: *Tour round North Wales*, 1798 (but several editions).

W. HUTTON: *North Wales*, 1803 (journeys in 1787, etc.).

DR SAMUEL JOHNSON: *Diary of a Journey into North Wales*, ed. R. Duppa, 1816. (A disappointing document.)

REV. JOHN PARKER: *The Passengers*, 1831.

GEORGE BORROW: *Wild Wales*, 1854. Many editions.

Borrow's was perhaps the last non-fictional book of absolutely general interest before *The Mountains of Snowdonia*, 1925. Edward Thomas's *Wales* (1905) has very beautiful passages, but little that is specifically Snowdonian.

The Climbers

W. P. HASKETT SMITH: *Climbing in the British Isles*, Part II, 1895.

G. D. and A. P. ABRAHAM: *Rock Climbing in North Wales*, 1906.

H. S. Salt: *On Cambrian and Cumbrian Hills,* 1906.

J. M. A. Thomson and A. W. Andrews: *The Climbs on Lliwedd,* 1909.

J. M. A. Thomson: *Climbing in the Ogwen District,* 1910.

H. R. Pope, in *Oxford Mountaineering Essays,* 1912.

A. Lunn: *The Mountains of Youth* (Cader Idris chapter), 1925.

H. R. C. Carr: *A Climber's Guide to Snowdon and the Beddgelert District,* 1926.

G. Winthrop Young: *On High Hills,* Chapter I, 1927.

C. E. Montague: *A Botanist in the Hanging Garden Gully* (from *Fiery Particles*), 1923.

> Various books from the late twenties onward, such as F. S. Smythe's *Climbs and Ski-Runs,* have important chapters on North Wales.   As referred to in text.

Climbers' Club Guide-books:

> *Cwm Idwal* by J. M. Edwards, 1936.
> *Tryfan* by J. M. Edwards and W. Noyce, 1937.
> *Glyder Fach* by C. F. Kirkus, 1937.
> *Lliwedd* by W. Noyce and J. M. Edwards, 1939.
> *Llanberis Pass* by P. R. J. Harding, 1950.
> *The Carneddau* by A. J. J. Moulam, 1953.
> Numerous articles from journals, references in text.

F. S. Smythe: *Over Welsh Hills* (the best book of photographs), 1940.

E. C. Pyatt and W. Noyce (ed.): *British Crags and Climbers,* 1952.

The Poets and Novelists

Thomas Gray: *The Bard,* 1755.

William Wordsworth: *The Prelude.*   Book XIV, 1805.

R. Southey: *Madoc in Wales,* 1805.

P. B. Shelley: various poems, *c.* 1812.

Thomas Love Peacock: *Headlong Hall,* 1815; *The Misfortunes of Elphin,* 1829.

George Meredith: *Poems.*

Charles Kingsley: *Two Years Ago,* 1857.

W. T. WATTS-DUNTON: *Aylwin*, 1898.

A. D. GODLEY: various verses (*c.* 1900).

LIONEL JOHNSON: *Poems* (various) (*c.* 1900).

G. WINTHROP YOUNG: *Freedom, Wind and Hill*, etc. All in *Collected Poems*, 1936.

WILLIAM BELL: *Mountains beneath the Horizon* (poems), 1950.

M. E. ALLAN: *School under Snowdon* (school story), 1950.

DOUGLAS HEWITT: *Mountain Rescue*, 1951.

ELIZABETH COXHEAD: *One Green Bottle*, 1951.

SHOWELL STYLES: *Death on Milestone Buttress*, 1951; *Land from the Sea*, 1952; *Death under Snowdon*, 1954; *Murder of an Owl*, 1956.

KEVIN FITZGERALD: *A Throne of Bayonets*, 1952; *It's Different in July*, 1955.

THOMAS FIRBANK: *I Bought a Mountain*, 1940, is not fiction, but perhaps points the way to more fiction.

History, Folklore, and Remains

Historia Britannorum (final form), 1810.

Mabinogion (over a period): translated by Lady Charlotte Guest in 1838, and by T. P. Ellis and J. Lloyd, 1929.

LEWIS MORRIS: *Celtic Remains*, Arch. Camb., 1878.

D. E. JENKINS: *Beddgelert, Its Facts, Fairies, and Folklore*, 1899.

SIR JOHN RHYS: *Celtic Folklore*, 1901.

Welsh Literature

ELIZABETH SHARP: *Lyra Celtica*, 1896.

W. HUGHES JONES: *At the Foot of Eryri*, 1912.

SIR IDRIS BELL: *Welsh Poetry*, 1936.

WILLIAM MORRIS: *Clychau Gwynedd* (the poem *Cwm Dyli*), 1946.

WILLIAM JONES: *Adar Rhiannon a Cherddi Eraill* (poems), 1947.

GWYN WILLIAMS: *An Introduction to Welsh Poetry*, 1953.

D. M. and E. M. LLOYD: *A Book of Wales* (pp. 76–86), 1953.

PARRY and BELL (ed.): *A History of Welsh Literature* (section on the twentieth century by Sir Idris Bell), 1955.

Science and Information

J. A. WALPOLE-BOND: *Bird Life in Wild Wales*, 2nd ed., 1915.

E. G. BILHAM: *Climate of the British Isles*, 1938.

M. DE C. S. SALTER: *Rainfall of the British Isles*, 1921.

H. R. C. CARR and G. A. LISTER (ed.): *The Mountains of Snowdonia*, 1925, 2nd ed., 1948.

F. J. NORTH, BRUCE CAMPBELL, RICHENDA SCOTT: *Snowdonia* (New Naturalist Series, 1949. Much information on geology, natural history, and historical background.)

Numerous papers in the *Quart. J. Geological Soc.*, by D. and H. Williams, W. G. Fearnside, W. Davies, etc.

INDEX

MAP OF SNOWDONIA

KEY TO NUMBERS

Snowdon Group

1. Clogwyn y Garnedd
2. Lliwedd
3. Crib Goch
4. Dinas Mot
5. Clogwyn y Ddysgl and y Person
6. Cyrn Las
7. Clogwyn du'r Arddu
8. Llechog

Glyder Group

9. The Three Cliffs
10. Craig Cwrwgl (Pillar of Elidir)
11. Creigiau Gleision
12. Twll Du (Devil's Kitchen)
13. Upper Cliff of Glyder Fawr
14. Idwal Slabs and Holly-tree Wall
15. Glyder Fach, Main Cliff
16. Tryfan, East Face

Carnedd Group

17. Llech Ddu
18. Ysgolion Duon (Black Ladders)
19. Craig yr Ysfa

Moel Siabod Group

20. Moel Siabod Cliff
21. Moelwyn and Moel yr Hydd Cliffs

Moel Hebog Group

22. Moel Hebog Cliffs
23. Craig y Bere
24. Craig Cwm Silyn
25. Tremadoc Rocks

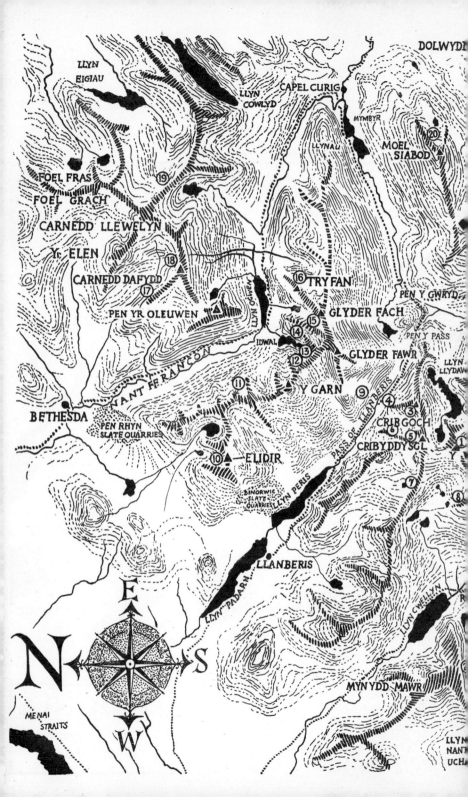